AL CAPONE

AL CAPONE

Rick Hornung

A Balliett & Fitzgerald Book

PARK LANE
NEW YORK

For Ben, who taught me how to beat the long odds
For Ruth, who taught me how to waltz at the Hotel Metropole

This 1998 edition is published by Park Lane Press,
a division of Random House Value Publishing, Inc.,
a Random House Company
201 East 50th Street, New York, New York 10022

A&E's acclaimed BIOGRAPHY series is available on videocassette from
A&E Home Video. Call 1-800-423-1212 to order.

A&E and **BIOGRAPHY** are trademarks of A&E Television Networks,
registered in the United States and other countries.

Park Lane Press and colophon are trademarks of
Random House Value Publishing, Inc.

Random House, Inc.
New York • Toronto • London • Sydney • Auckland
www.randomhouse.com

Printed and bound in the United States of America

A Balliett & Fitzgerald Book
Series Editor: Thomas Dyja
Book Design: Lisa Govan, Susan Canavan
Production Editors: Maria Fernandez, Mike Walters
Photo Research: Maria Fernandez
Assistant Editor: Irene Agriodimas

Library of Congress Cataloging-in-Publication Data

Hornung, Rick.
    Al Capone / Rick Hornung.   —1st ed.
        p.   cm.   —(Biography)
    "A Balliett & Fitzgerald book."
        Includes bibliographical (p. 171) references and index.
        1. Capone, Al, 1899–1947. 2. Criminals—Illinois—Chicago—
    Biography. 3. Organized crime—Illinois—Chicago—History.
    I. Title.   II. Series: Biography (Park Lane Press)
    HV6248.C17H67   1998
    364.1'092—dc21
    (B)   98-20059
                                                                      CIP
    ISBN 0-517-20100-3
    10 9 8 7 6 5 4 3 2 1
    First Edition

CONTENTS

Capone at his peak.

CHAPTER ONE

YOUNG ALPHONSE

---◆---

T he family left Naples intact: a husband and wife, their three-year-old boy Vincenzo, standing on his own but clutching his father's hand, the infant son Raffaele, swaddled in the bosom of his pregnant mother. Arriving at Ellis Island and stepping into the maze of holding rooms and customs counters, immigration inspectors and health examiners, they relied on the patriarch, thirty-year-old Gabriele, to fill out the forms in his own hand. Unlike the majority of the 42,977 Italians who arrived in 1894 and sought legal residency in the United States, he had brought enough money to pursue his goal of building his own business.

Once officials cleared their papers and allowed the family to pass, Gabriele already knew enough about New York to avoid the notorious section of Mulberry Bend in lower Manhattan, where thousands of Italian immigrants were crowded into tenements and shepherded to work in construction gangs controlled by extortionate padrones. Instead of throwing his family into the island's cauldron of ethnic groups, he sought out the small enclave of Neapolitans wedged between the Gowanus Canal and Brooklyn's bustling docks, where a flat without plumbing rented for three and a half or four dollars per month.

Eager to take advantage of the commerce generated by the nearby Navy Yard, Gabriele opened a grocery, but by the time Teresina gave birth to their third son, Salvatore—the first Capone born in America—Gabriele had returned to the trade he learned in Naples: cutting hair.

The business provided a steady income in a community that was constantly striving to mix and match its southern Italian ways with America's grinding growth. Most Neapolitan men were shut out of the Navy Yard's workforce of Irish and German immigrants, so they found jobs on the tunnel gangs, stone-cutting crews, loading docks, and metal shops that were constructing a city. For wages that averaged less than $150 per year, Italian men were repeatedly ridiculed by the employers who were paying them twenty to forty percent less than other immigrant groups.

Into this close-knit world of hustle and hard work, the fourth Capone son, Alphonse, was born. Like all of his brothers, he came to life full of robust health. A chubby infant who arrived with large shoulders, thick torso, but short legs and small hands—physical characteristics that would define him for the rest of his life—the child was welcomed by his father as a sign of well-being and stability in the family's new homeland.

When Gabriele and Teresina brought Alphonse to St. Michael and St. Edward's altar for his baptism on February 7, 1899, the family of six had reached what many congregants considered to be unbridled prosperity: Besides owning a business at the new address of 69 Park Avenue, the Capones lived in the same building. The new century brought continued growth as Gabriele and Teresina sought a daughter for their brood of sons. While the two eldest boys attended P.S. 7 on nearby Adams Street, Teresina started to supplement the family income by taking in seamstress work, an activity that continued throughout the pregnancy that delivered a fifth boy, Erminio, in 1901. With a family of seven to support and a business to operate, Gabriele took yet another step up the ladder of respectability, by buying the building that housed his barber shop and moving to a series of larger apartments on Garfield Place, a residential street.

A year after the 1903 completion of the Williamsburg Bridge, five-year-old Alphonse followed his brothers to school, learning the neighborhood boundaries marked by the rattle of the Myrtle Avenue El, the Navy Yard's 100-ton floating crane, the bazaar of tattoo parlors, gaming dens, dance halls, taverns, and pawnshops that broke down Sands Street after it sliced away from Navy Street. One of his earliest teachers, Sadie Mulvaney, then a sixteen-year-old fresh from training by Catholic nuns, called him "swarthy, sullen," a big and strong Italian kid nicknamed "Macaroni" by the taunting Irish boys.

When Gabriele Capone appeared at the Kings County Courthouse to be sworn into citizenship on May 25, 1906, all of his sons were enrolled in school, speaking English, and learning the ways of America. The birth of Umberto made the boy the sixth in a stable of boys, but the 1908 birth of a seventh son, Amedeo, disrupted the family. The eldest son, Vincenzo, ran away, unwilling to shoulder the burdens of school or keeping track of his brothers. Beyond the Mississippi, where his darkly complected face was tabbed as the countenance of a half-breed Sioux or Mexican, Vincenzo jumped into his new identity as Richard James Hart, earning his keep as a carnival roustabout who shot whiskey bottles out of the air and wrestled in sideshows.

The first Capone daughter was born nearly a year after he left Brooklyn. A sickly child who tested the emotional reserves of a large family, Rose required almost all of her mother's attention, but nothing could rescue the baby from an unknown illness that ended her life before her first birthday. Despite the tragedy, Gabriele and Teresina pressed on for a girl—the mother relying on the oldest boys, Raffaele and Salvatore, to look after their brothers.

Though family members referred to them by their Italian names, classmates and friends, teachers and prospective employers preferred English. The pudgy, oval-faced Raffaele easily became Ralph and the barrel-chested Alphonse took on Al, the lean Salvatore adopted Frank, wiry Umberto turned into Albert, roly-poly Erminio grew into John, and lanky Amedoe evolved to Matthew. Despite Teresina's old-world habits and Gabriele's avid participation in Neapolitan civic groups, the Capone boys embraced the world offered by Brooklyn's wide-open docks and tightly bent corners. They joined with other transplanted sons of Naples to run as the Navy Street Boys, a group that took on the Gowanus Dukes or Red Hook Rippers. At one point, Al's teasing of a Navy Yard guard resulted in the dismissal of a detail and the face-to-face taunting of a Marine sergeant. Another occasion found Al and the Navy Street Boys in a showdown with the Havermeyer Streeters, a Williamsburg-based group of Jewish toughs who smashed windows of Christian mission houses.

As part of his foray into the streets, Al manned a shoe-shine stand near the docks and eventually crossed the river to the financial district of Manhattan. Al's enterprising spirit and hard work prompted jealousy among other bootblacks. According to his friend Jack Woodford, Capone's stand became the target of threats. After he had posted himself in the lobby of a downtown Brooklyn bank, Capone took the short end of a beating but managed to protect his turf.

A few weeks later, he moved to the lobby of a Wall Street building, setting up his chair on stilts. Within days, a group that included a distant relative smashed the stand and challenged Al to a fight. He had no chance against six or seven. "When he found the broken legs of his chair, this was the end of the world," Woodford noted in his memoir *My Years with Capone*.

"Al became thoroughly anti-social. He went to the police and the police pushed him away, and from that time on, he had no respect for the police. He was a Dago kid who came from the wharves of Brooklyn, so the police weren't interested in helping him. That's how Al came to think as he did. Then, he became a street brawler."

To many who would come to know the gangster Al Capone, the destruction of his shoe-shine chair served as a turning point in his life. At that moment, the young Al realized that brute force could shatter a person's will. While many writers and biographers would eventually attribute Al's thuggery and drastic brutality to personality disorders, mental instability, or brain damage due to untreated syphilis, his friends, rivals, colleagues, and cohorts saw the source of his explosive rage in the events that demolished his shoe-shine stand.

Though young Al had honorably pursued an honest job, his efforts had been reduced to a heap. Faced with humiliation and defeat, the boy refused to place himself in yet another position of vulnerability. In his preadolescent mind, hard work and legitimate enterprise would lead only to another beating, something Al could not face. It was better to victimize than be the victim. This simple, street-corner proposition became the foundation of his life.

By the time Al was enrolled in sixth grade at P.S. 133, he had begun a pattern of truancy and fell behind in arithmetic and grammar. As his brother Ralph had before him, Al flunked

"Little John" Torrio, Capone's lifelong mentor in crime.

sixth grade and had to endure the shame of repeating the year. His absences skyrocketed, with 33 days missed out of a possible 90 in one marking period. The delinquency, however, did not draw any serious reproach from his parents or older brothers, who were busy: Ralph, who had quit school, punched the clock; studious Frank hit the books; and his parents prepared for yet another pregnancy—the ninth, which they hoped would produce a daughter.

❖   ❖   ❖

". . . a fella in need."

On January 28, 1912, ten days after Al's thirteenth birthday, Teresina Capone went into labor and gave birth to another girl. Ecstatic over this healthy and relatively easy delivery, mother and father anointed their prize with the name of Mafalda, in honor of a princess from a Neapolitan folktale. While Gabriele offered cigars and decorated his barber shop for a feast, Teresina focused on the child she had always wanted.

The Capone boys were on their own.

Everybody in the neighborhood knew Little John Torrio, the slender, mild-mannered man in his thirties who worked out of a second-story office above the corner of Fourth Avenue and Union Street. A native of Naples, John Torrio came to New York in the 1880s, finding his way to Manhattan, when the notorious Five Points gang ran parts of the Lower East Side according to the rules of eye-gouging and skull-bashing. While enlisting a boxer named Paolo Antonini Vacarelli to handle the muscular aspects of street life, the soft-spoken, delicately built Torrio took care of the thinking: With Vacarelli's help, he organized the first Italian leadership of the gang.

GANGS AND FIVE POINTS

A young boy like Al Capone, growing up in Brooklyn, could not roam without crossing territory staked out by a network of gangs and hustlers. These groups defending neighborhoods and street corners were seen as proving grounds for the few outfits that reached throughout New York and muscled their way into a variety of rackets. For more than a century, the most notorious gang was centered in the "Bloody Ould Sixth Ward" between Broadway and the Bowery in lower Manhattan. Initially known as the Forty Thieves, it was transformed into the Shirt Tails—so named because its members wore their shirttails outside their trousers. Throughout the first decades of the nineteenth century, this gang consolidated its hold on Manhattan's vice trade and moved north with the expansion of the city. The first wave of Irish immigrants created the Plug Uglies, whose members bludgeoned their victims and stamped them to death with nailed boots. An offshoot of this combat turned into the Dead Rabbits, a group of ruffians who fought behind a standard-bearer carrying a dead rabbit stuck on a spear.

After the Civil War, these groups were consolidated into a multiethnic outfit known as the Whyos, who printed up a price list: Two dollars for punching and one hundred dollars for "doing the job." Out of the Whyos came the Five Pointers, a group of 1,500 that ran every establishment in the territory bounded by Broadway, the Bowery, City Hall, and 14th Street.

With the city's expansion and the gang leadership's desire to help local political candidates round up voters, the Five Pointers returned to intraethnic rivalries, and Italians and Irish fought for control. Though this feud led to a decline in membership and a purge of the Irish, it also allowed Italian gangsters to filter throughout New York and open their own enterprises as a front for lotteries, prostitution, extortion, and loan-sharking.

"This band of hooligans wreaks more terror than any other," claimed Police Commissioner Theodore Roosevelt. "They are the biggest threat to decency and respect for law in any part of our city. These young men infect our streets with violence, public lewdness and any vice known to humanity."

Torrio broke down the Five Pointers into turfs that minimized competition and maximized profits, bringing New York's leading organization of leg-breakers and extortionists into the twentieth century.

As a reward, Torrio was given control of Jane Street, where he refined the skills needed to run numbers. When Greenwich Village reformers cracked down and insisted that Mayor Seth Low clean up their neighborhood by constructing a police station in the middle of Sixth Avenue, Torrio showed the smarts that would bless his career for decades. Instead of slugging it out, he moved to a new turf.

Brooklyn was wide open. Torrio used the numbers to finance his stake in the Sands Street strip of gaming dens and cathouses. As his business grew and multiplied his need for runners, the diminutive Torrio enlisted one of the many neighborhood boys to come upstairs, where a two-dollar bill would be offered in exchange for an hour of work. If you were loyal and performed well in the first few tasks, Little John offered you a chance at even more money. Though Ralph Capone had a legitimate job at a book bindery, he was the first family member to seek Torrio's help in finding a second source of income: Once Ralph passed the loyalty test, Little John obliged, arranging for the boy to pick up soda pop empties in the neighborhood grocery stores, ice-cream parlors, diners, and taverns. In honor of this service, neighborhood boys tagged Ralph with a new name—"Bottles."

The broad-shouldered Al grew bolder in his streetside exploits, but rising frustration with teachers and principals triggered the outburst that steered him to Torrio: Having barely made it to the seventh grade in 1913, Al found himself the subject of needling by peers and condescension from the teacher. When she gave a lesson that exposed his failings to the class, Capone lashed out, hurling a string of foulmouthed epithets. To Capone's surprise, the teacher struck him. Drawing on the lesson of the shoe-shine stand, the young Al Capone refused to let any teacher play him for a chump. He slugged her, thereby committing his first publicly recorded act of violent disobedience. When the principal was informed, he took the fourteen-year-old into his office and laid on a beating.

At home, Alphonse vowed never to return to P.S. 133. His parents supported the decision as long as their fourth son found a job and brought home money.

Al went to Little John Torrio, who knew how to put boys to work. His gang would help a fella in need.

John Torrio's first step in educating his new protégé was a quick course explaining how to use a legitimate job to cover extra cash generated from collections, payouts, parlays, and juice: By arranging straight wages of three bucks per week for Al, Torrio instructed the fourteen-year-old to honor his parents and turn over a needed paycheck to help defray the expenses of raising four younger brothers and a sister. When the eager teen showed a desire to earn a bit for himself, Torrio assigned Al illicit tasks that would demonstrate his loyalty and reliability.

On the legit, Al held the counter at a snack shop at 305 Fifth Avenue, drawing a salary. At the same time, however, he stepped into a network of vice that covered northwest Brooklyn and reached across the Williamsburg Bridge into lower Manhattan, where Torrio still had allies in the Five Pointers. After a day of tending to customers and making sure they could place bets in the back of the store, Capone was frequently dispatched to settle outstanding accounts or deliver winnings—a job that gave Torrio a chance to assess the youngster's potential in the racket. Like many others working for Torrio, young Al competed for his boss's attention by bringing back as much money as possible. Though Ralph Capone had shown Torrio enough moxie to keep and expand his bottle route, Al enjoyed a scrape, proving himself capable with fists, wooden clubs, and a blackjack.

Al's initial success prompted a few of the older hoods to tell Torrio that Capone was cheating the gang. To test the boy, Little John summoned Capone to his Fourth Avenue office. Spreading a roll of currency on the table as if intending to count it, Little John suddenly dashed away. Upon his return, he found Capone sitting just where he had left him. All of the money remained.

After Capone proved his loyalty, Torrio arranged for the boy to have a new legitimate job as a pinsetter in a bowling alley. Following Torrio's advice, fifteen-year-old Capone refused to let his mother and father know of his second job or the source of any extra income. In a lesson that would become the cornerstone of gangland life, Torrio insisted on a clean and straight family life for Capone and any other young man seeking to earn the wages of sin. He knew that his business depended on trustworthy employees: If a young man could not honor his own family, then he could not be dependable.

Many Sands Street grifters knew Capone as an ambitious thug who served on Torrio's crew, but his neighbors in the sedate strip of apartments that lined Garfield Place had the opposite impression. Daniel Fuchs, one of the earliest novelists to write about Jewish immigrant life in Brooklyn, grew up a few blocks south of Capone and came to know him as "something of a non-entity." Another neighborhood kid who grew up to be a writer, Edward Dean Sullivan, recalled that the teenage Capone "never drank and the one outstanding trait known about him, in the tough circles where his skill with a cue won him some attention, was that he must be home every night at 10:30."

Adding to the young Capone's persona was his appetite for fine clothes, a taste acquired from Torrio. As he began to earn more, Al enjoyed showing it off—pleated woolen pants, colorful sweaters and jackets, and brightly colored shirts. Pleased that neighbors and his fellow hoods took notice, the teen also began to have fun: With his father, Al frequented the pool hall on the corner of Garfield Place, and with his pals from Torrio's gang, he often slipped into a dance hall or cathouse high-stepping his way through showgirls and sideshow attractions. Fuchs remembered Capone as "an excellent dancer."

❖ ❖ ❖

"Scarface"

As an ambitious sixteen-year-old apprentice in the vice trade, Al was eager for a promotion. Having won the trust of Torrio, he sought assignments that would take him beyond Brooklyn and into Manhattan for contact with other gangs. Along with former schoolyard chum Salvatore Lucania—later to be infamous as Lucky Luciano—Capone was given the task of solidifying Torrio's link to remnants of the Five Pointers, which had been reorganized and nearly disbanded as the result of a brutal war between the Italian leadership under the control of the urbane ex-bantamweight Paolo Antonini Vacarelli, a deadly Irish bon vivant known as Biff Ellison, and the skull-cracking Jewish gangster Monk Eastmann. As these ethnic groups locked into a leg-breaking, gun-toting competition for control of Manhattan, Torrio weighed in behind his Italian paisan Vacarelli.

From the feuds that tore open Manhattan, the young Capone received a firsthand glimpse of how many gangs relied on the old-world Black Hand methods of extortion, violence, and intimidation to defend their turf. At the same time, he saw how Torrio used the opposite approach in Brooklyn, where compromise, negotiation, and attention to neighborhood and family removed the perception of a gangster's menace. Throughout northwestern Brooklyn where Neapolitan, Calabrian, and Tuscan immigrants choked the streets, Torrio worked to earn the respect and goodwill of his community. He made sure the carnival atmosphere of Sands Street did not spill over to the rows of tenements that served as home to hardworking men, their wives, and their children.

As the battle for Manhattan wound down and gave Little John Torrio's ally, Vacarelli, a chance to expand uptown, Lucania showed his initiative: He asked Little John for permission to forsake Brooklyn and step into the leadership vacuum on the Lower East Side between 14th Street and City Hall, the Bowery to Broadway. Little John offered his blessings to Lucania and continued Al's apprenticeship by sending him to work in a South Brooklyn clubhouse operated by a notorious enforcer, Joe Adonis, who ran his joint as a front for young men seeking to learn pistol skills.

Although Europe's war brought a boom of economic activity to the Brooklyn Navy Yard and nearby docks, the ever-enterprising Torrio had focused elsewhere for his next step. Instead of slugging it out in the increasingly contested streets of New York, Little John took an offer put forth by his uncle, Jim "Big Jim" Colosimo, proprietor of a Chicago café that catered to crooked pols, gamblers, hookers, highbrow society on the prowl for sin, opera singers, and burlesque bon vivants. With the 1915 election of Mayor William "Big Bill" Thompson ushering in an unprecedented era of graft and greed, Big Jim offered Little John a chance to become business manager of

Joe Adonis, owner of the club where Capone learned how to shoot.

the Windy City's hottest nightspot. From Colosimo's Café, Little John could effectively weave Chicago's underworld into the fabric of the city's political life. In New York, Little John clearly would always have to keep two steps ahead of his rivals and one step ahead of the law; in Chicago, Big Jim presented the possibility of consolidating competition into a cartel and cutting in the cops and city hall as partners.

Torrio accepted the proposition and headed west. As he began the process of relocating and disbanding his Brooklyn organization, Torrio furthered his plans for Capone's apprenticeship by introducing the teenage hood to one of the borough's most feared racketeers, Frankie Yale. Born in Calabria as Francesco Ioele, he came to the United States as a young boy in 1893, and settled in lower Manhattan's Mulberry Bend. He joined the Five Point Juniors, rising in prominence when such Italians as Torrio and Vacarelli made their move. After surviving the battles between Irish, Italian, and Jewish gangs, Ioele had learned enough about New York to recast himself as Frankie Yale and find open turf in south Brooklyn.

With his Surf Avenue headquarters converted into a night-club, Frankie needed a muscular kid who could serve as bar-tender and bouncer, errand boy and part-time stage manager or waiter. For a candidate, Frankie turned to his pal Johnny Torrio, who recommended Capone.

The timing was perfect: Al had the right personality and skills for high life. While Yale planted himself at a table and reviewed the day's ice or cigar haul with his sidekick "Little Augie" Carafano, young Al tended to customers, drawing beer and waiting on tables, scrubbing the long bar or taking a turn on the dance floor.

Though Yale clearly enjoyed Capone's desire to mingle with customers and show them a good time, the boss became con-cerned when the eighteen-year-old couldn't take his eyes off the voluptuous sister of Frankie Gallucio, a wiry, gut-bucket-tough, second-story man. As Capone eagerly flirted with the girl, Yale grew nervous, hoping his employee would not pro-voke a fight. Capone leaned over her shoulder and told her, "Honey, you have a nice ass, and I mean that as a compli-ment." Gallucio sprang to his feet and pounded his left fist into Capone's stomach; at the same time, Gallucio's right hand whipped open a knife and his arm extended—once, twice, thrice. Within seconds, Capone's blood sprayed across the dance floor. Gallucio and his sister ran.

After Capone's wounds were stitched, he went to Yale for help in seeking revenge. But his boss remained less than sympathetic, so Capone appealed to Torrio's allies Albert Altieri and Salvatore Lucania. When they failed to support Capone's bid for retribution, the parties agreed to a face-to-face meeting on Surf Avenue. With his safety guaranteed, Gallucio decided to attend and apologize for cutting Capone's face. At the same time, Capone had to admit that he understood and honored Gallucio's need to protect his sister.

As a result of the compromise, Yale agreed to keep Capone on his payroll. Within weeks, the wounds healed, leaving three thick lines on the left side of Capone's face—the first rounding his cheek for four inches, the second curving with his jaw for two inches, and the third hooked onto his neck beneath the earlobe.

To a number of Capone's streetfighting buddies, the marks were a badge of honor. But he knew that his face was scarred for life.

❧ ❧ ❧

"... a kid who had to learn how to hustle for himself."

The disfigurement did not prevent the eighteen-year-old Capone from chasing a variety of girls and women. According to medical records that were compiled later in Capone's life, his carousing led to an early bout with venereal disease, which went untreated. Though many Capone biographers—most recently Laurence Bergreen—claim that improperly treated syphilis would eventually cause or contribute to Al's instabil-

Brooklyn mobster Frankie Yale, a sometime ally, sometime rival of Capone.

ity and mental decline, his attempts to cure himself followed common practice during the early twentieth century.

Despite the widespread occurrence of this illness, it remained a secret for millions of men and women who refused to seek treatment. As Bergreen documents in his book *Capone: The Man and the Era*, Al handled his own illness and went about his ways unaware that his youthful encounters would cause a harsh and devastating return of the syphilis in his later years. Throughout his extensive research, Bergreen makes a strong case that the teenager never fully rid himself of the disease. While Bergreen speculates that the effects of latent syphilis contributed to Capone's later outbursts and flashpoints of anger, many of the gangster's contemporaries and colleagues, his rivals and his pursuers, discount disease as the source of Al's explosive use of violence. To his peers, Capone's demonic behavior was part of a pattern designed to increase his underworld standing.

"From the beginning, he was a kid looking to be beat on his way up into the rackets," commented legendary newspaperman Ben Hecht, who used Capone as a model in his script for *Scarface*, the classic gangster movie. "Al wasn't a psychopath or someone really nuts, but a kid who had to learn how to hustle for himself. That's what steered him into trouble. He figured he could handle anything. Cut all the angles."

Believing that he had conquered the clap, Capone continued his encounters with prostitutes and flappers. Known on the streets as a pool shark and Coney Island bouncer, two-bit gambler and quick-fisted enforcer, Al Capone had engineered a small following for himself.

On Garfield Place, he was delighted by the company of the vivacious Domenicia, a girl of thirteen or fourteen known as Susie. She was impressed by the free-spending ways of the young man on the way up, and eager to be on his arm. Susie's easygoing temperament drew Al's attention and pleased him. But Gabriele and Teresina saw the romance in terms of the tradition of Naples, and they called on the girl's parents to see if the match was acceptable. The Capones' fellow immigrants surprised them, dismissing Al and insisting that the romance be stopped.

Unwilling to disobey, Al returned to courtships made in the shadows of his work. "He thought prostitutes were the easier way," recalled Jack Woodford. "The least troublesome thing was to pay for it and walk out." To facilitate these dalliances, he joined his peers in a few cellar clubs—basement joints that gave young men and women space to meet and socialize without the formalities of commercial establishments. Sprinkled throughout the borough, these clubhouses were usually a rented storefront or the storage space beneath the street operated by a group of young men or a neighborhood association. The entertainment featured a local piano player, an off-duty chorus girl, a couple of roulette tables, and what was often believed to be a loaded dice game. Capone came to be a regular on Carroll Street, where Irish and Italians had negotiated their way into a truce.

At one of these clubs, Al met a slim, high-cheekboned blonde who caught the eye of many local hoods. Mary Coughlin, known as Mae, appeared to be the exact opposite of a tough guy's moll: A high school graduate who held down a regular job at a local department store, she came from a devout family that openly supported a number of Irish associations in their neighborhood south of Brooklyn Heights. "Mae was different from the other girls Al had known," writes Bergreen. "She was older than he, not a child, but an adult . . . she came from another culture, the world of middle class respectability." While Capone and his peers could race through the borough's underworld and pick women from show business and bordellos, he became focused on a proper courtship to a good-looking woman from a respectable family. Besides his physical attraction for Mae and the thrill of having an older, established girl fall for him, Capone saw this relationship as a chance to incorporate one of Little John Torrio's cardinal lessons for being a successful hood—the creation of a solid domestic life.

Unlike other women, Mae did not need a marriage proposal or an illicit business arrangement to engage in sexual relations; she enjoyed lovemaking without a promise to marry or a commitment to monogamy. Within months, she was pregnant.

Despite their daughter's condition, the Coughlins did not demand an end to the romance, and Mae continued to be with the father of her unborn child. Capone was thrilled to be accepted by a grown woman whose family had prospered on coming to America, and he began to consider the possibility of leaving the rackets and crossing over to legitimacy. While his career as a bouncer and muscle man led the police to arrest him once for disorderly conduct and twice for suspicion of homicide, there was no evidence to support any of the charges—surely his clean record would qualify him for the straight life. When the Selective Service issued an ultimatum requiring him to report on September 12, 1918, Capone appeared and registered for the draft. He learned that his only possibility for an exemption was marriage.

Mae was his choice, not Uncle Sam.

To avoid a wedding ceremony while Mae was obviously pregnant, the families decided to wait until after the delivery. With the blessings of the Rev. James J. Delaney of St. Mary Star of the Sea, Al Capone married in the church, on December 30, 1918. Mae's oldest sister was a bridesmaid and witness, and her parents sat in the first pew across the aisle from Gabriele, Teresina, and Al's siblings. As the newlyweds took their vows, their three-week-old son, Albert Francis, was cradled in the arms of relatives.

Mae, a.k.a. Mary Coughlin. In 1918, she became Mrs. Al Capone.

When the boy was baptized, Little John Torrio came from Chicago to stand as godfather.

Shortly after the marriage, Capone found himself in his first serious jam with the law. Though he spent more time thinking about a day job and spending nights at home with bride and son, Frankie Yale still offered the opportunity to earn fast cash through collections, standing guard over a few crooked dice games, and running errands. "How else could he [Al] make a living?" recounted Woodford. "He couldn't just go in to an ordinary employer and say, 'Look, I left school and I shined shoes and I have been a body guard. What have you got in my line?'" To Capone, this easy cash could not be passed up. He figured it could finance his decision to move away from Brooklyn and make a fresh start.

In the early months of 1919, Yale found that he had been repeatedly shorted by a Brooklyn grifter named Tony Perotta. After Yale issued a series of warnings, he commissioned Capone to collect on an outstanding balance of $1,500. Having known Perotta through the borough's network of gaming dens, Capone found his mark at a crap game run by one of Yale's rivals. As he approached Perotta with a demand for payment, Capone anticipated some resistance and applied force, but violence did not persuade Perotta to come up with the money. As the confrontation escalated, Al lost his temper. Before Perotta could summon help, Al drew his pistol and fired, killing a man for the first time.

Though Capone made sure to collect some money off the corpse, Yale wasn't interested: He knew the cops would be looking for his trusted enforcer. Capone had to hide.

Capone went to Baltimore with Mae and Albert Francis, now affectionately called "Sonny," relying on his Brooklyn connections to arrange an office job with the Aiello Construction Company, an upright, aboveboard business that focused on building houses and lending money to new owners. Capone quietly managed the ledgers of the family-owned business, posting payables and receivables. Though clerical work in Baltimore seemed tedious and drab compared to the rowdy street assignments of Brooklyn, Capone accepted regular hours and went through the motions of being a family man. Despite the obvious gaps in his formal education, he was a quick study and learned how to tabulate profit margins, debits, rollbacks, credits, rent schedules, lease schedules, and mortgage rates. For the first time in his life, he could call himself a legitimate success.

That satisfaction, however, would last less than a year. In 1920, Gabriele Capone grew ill and his wife sought financial help from Al. Aware that Ralph and Al had dabbled in thug life while Frank remained in school and pursued a legitimate career in business, she urged the older boys to pool their extra cash and send it to Brooklyn. But her sons recognized that a bookkeeper, an insurance salesman, and a student could not earn enough to support themselves, their wives, their children, an infirm father, a mother, and three siblings. When Gabriele died on November 14, 1920, the entire family—except Vincenzo—gathered at Garfield Place. Facing the possibility of their mother and siblings sliding into poverty, Al and Ralph made their choice; a hustler's life could meet the need for extra money.

Once again, Al turned to the man who had always helped— John Torrio. Aware that the outstanding murder probe would hinder Al's ability to work in New York, Torrio offered him a job in Chicago. With his new family's blessing, Al accepted.

Twenty-two-year-old Al boarded a train for the Midwest in early 1921, and Mae and Sonny headed north to Brooklyn, where they were to live on Garfield Place until the new head of the Capone family had settled into the "city of big shoulders."

Capone, hiding his scar

CHAPTER TWO

CAPONE COMES TO CHICAGO

———◆———

W hen Al Capone stepped off the train at Chicago's Union Station, he stood less than two miles north of the red-light district that would lead him to a life of infamy. Known as the Levee—a sixteen-square-block rectangle of whorehouses, taverns, burlesque palaces, and gaming parlors that catered to all strata of the city's life—this open bazaar of vice became the young man's introduction to a Chicago that bought and sold power, privilege, and prestige.

Stepping into this quadrant, Capone became aware that John Torrio had spent years quietly weaving a network of graft, extortion, violence, intimidation, and bribery. While Capone knew of Torrio's talents only in Brooklyn, he soon learned that his patron came to Chicago to shape the underworld organization of Big Jim Colosimo, the man who once dominated the Levee and its enterprises. Colosimo was involved with dozens of brothels, white slavers, gin joints, and gaming dens, but he needed Torrio to integrate the operation into an enterprise. Torrio's first step was to arrange for the shotgunning of Colosimo's chief competitor, Sunny Jim Cosmano; then, he initiated a strict and regular system of bribery, because payoffs were just another cost of doing business. To solidify Colosimo's control over the Levee and strengthen his organization, Torrio made sure that all of the politicians received their payola from him. Once Colosimo's organization bought the loyalty of the Levee's political overlords, John Joseph "Bathhouse" Coughlin and Michael "Hinky Dink" Kenna, the vice racket quickly expanded into a mixture of politics and extortion.

As Colosimo stepped away from the day-to-day operation of the vice business and fancied himself an influence peddler who reached into the office of Mayor William "Big Bill" Thompson, he refused to focus on Torrio's predictions that the sale of liquor would be the next wave of illicit trade.

Preoccupied with a new romance with a nineteen-year-old singer named Dale Winter, Colosimo wasn't giving Torrio the attention needed to consolidate the patchwork network of breweries, distillers, truckers, and haulers needed to caravan beer and booze once the Volstead Act, or Prohibition, was passed on January 1, 1920. To fill Chicago's enormous thirst, many suppliers came through Canada to the United States by way of Detroit; others slipped into Wisconsin or Minnesota and drove south. But a critical route involved Torrio's old pal from Coney Island, Frankie Yale, who received his stock from seaborne runners. Using his knowledge of Brooklyn's wharves and warehouses, Frankie easily arranged for trucks to be loaded and sent west through New Jersey, Pennsylvania, Ohio, Indiana, and finally into Chicago's southeast side.

On May 11, 1920, the seventh day of his marriage to

Winter, Big Jim Colosimo received a phone call from Torrio, who told him of a whiskey shipment scheduled to arrive at the café around 4 P.M. After spending most of the day with his bride, Colosimo pinned a red rose in his lapel, placed a homburg on his head, and walked into his restaurant.

For twenty-five minutes, Colosimo spoke with his secretary and the chef, then went for the glass doors that opened toward the street. Moments before, a porter had noticed a stranger sneaking into the vestibule's phone booth. When Colosimo passed by, two shots rang out and he collapsed onto his back.

Police Chief John J. Garrity was among the first to arrive; he saw the wounds behind Colosimo's right ear. Though the cops would question scores of suspects, the porter provided the best lead: In a book of mug shots, he identified Frankie Yale as the stranger who had lurked in the café's telephone booth. But after the New York cops picked up Yale, the porter had second thoughts about giving his testimony.

Yale was never charged, and Little John Torrio figured that he himself needed a bodyguard. If his former pal could hit Big Jim, then Little John should not be unprotected. So he found Capone and offered him a job, knowing that the young man who had grown up in Yale's shadow would be the perfect choice.

❧ ❧ ❧

"a wounded water buffalo"

Residing in a small, unpretentious flat overlooking the quiet northside intersection of Sheridan Road and Falwell Street, Capone found himself in a working-class neighborhood of six flats recently built to accommodate the bursting metropolis that had grown from 500,000 citizens in 1880 to 2.7 mil-

BIG JIM COLOSIMO

Big Jim Colosimo, the first crime lord of Chicago.

When James "Big Jim" Colosimo arrived in Chicago, the seventeen-year-old son of Naples started with a shoe-shine stand. A year later, in 1896, he was hauling water for railroad crews that began to lay tracks through the first ward, the domain of political overlords John Joseph "Bathhouse" Coughlin and Michael "Hinky Dink" Kenna. As aldermen and political bosses, this duo demanded a cut of all the economic activity, and they used the strapping Colosimo to carry the bag.

Impressed with his ability to intimidate, Coughlin and Kenna steered Big Jim to their vice businesses: He pimped at night and served as foreman of a city street-sweeping crew by day. To show his gratitude, Colosimo organized a social club of Italian immigrants who pumped the Levee and surrounding districts for votes.

With Coughlin and Kenna in his corner, Big Jim took on a number of jobs: poolroom manager, saloonkeeper, and delivery man for bribes paid by whoremasters and pimps. On his appointed rounds, Colosimo met Victoria Moresco, a middle-aged madam who owned her own house, a second-tier bordello on the fringes of the Levee. Eager to use his youthful energy and ambition to improve her business, Moresco offered Big Jim the job as manager, which became the first step toward their marriage.

They combined his brawn and political connections with her recruiting skills. With Bathhouse John and Hinky Dink guiding business opportunities toward Big Jim, he improved Moresco's operation, renaming it the Victoria and outfitting it with posh furniture and younger women. To keep his hands on the lucrative trade for lower-paying customers, Colosimo opened his own house, where the price remained under two dollars. The modest tariff proved to be a recipe for success; Colosimo expanded his operations, acquiring existing houses and turning two or three family apartment buildings into cribs for the Levee's night crawlers.

By 1908, Colosimo and Moresco had become trapped in a web of payoffs and protection rackets that required drastic action. To reorganize the riff-raff shakedowns he had once mastered for Coughlin and Kenna, Big Jim summoned his nephew John Torrio from Brooklyn. With his help, Big Jim arranged the shotgunning of a rival hood and then instituted a systematic payroll for crooked cops and pols.

As Torrio shuttled back and forth from Brooklyn, Big Jim continued to expand his operations, converting a Wabash Avenue warehouse into a spectacular eatery: The walls were decked in green velvet; gilded frames surrounded the oval windows; crystal chandeliers hung from a pale blue ceiling adorned with pink-faced angels and rose-tinted clouds; and mirrors stood behind the mahogany-and-glass bar.

When it was time for entertainment or dancing at Colosimo's Café, a series of hydraulic winches and lifts elevated the wooden floor or stage, giving performers and patrons a chance to enjoy an aria from *Aïda* or a rousing chorus of "Oh! How She Could Yacki, Hacki, Wicki, Wacki, Woo!" With Big Jim serving as a roving host who could boast of connections to the world-famous tenor Enrico Caruso or local crap player Jules "Lovin' Putty" Annixter, the café quickly turned into a sensation that attracted all types of Chicagoans. "Here they could rub elbows with demimondaines and their pimps," wrote successful mayoral candidate Carter Harrison Jr., the leader of Chicago's reform movement, "with gamblers, prize fighters, liquor agents and out and out sex perverts."

lion by 1920. The city's political geography followed the turn of the Chicago River and its two branches: To the south, checkerboard squares of houses and tenements were pitched upon the flats, alternating blacks and Irish, Italians and Croats, Serbs and Poles. At the center lay the mammoth stockyards, where 75,000 people worked each day and slaughtered more than 17 million animals each year. To the north, posh brownstones and neo-Gothic high-rises were bisected by meridians that ran to Milwaukee or Kankakee, extending the sprawl of Irish along Clark Street, Germans up and down Lincoln Avenue, and Swedes and Finns in Andersonville. To the west, clusters of Jews and Poles were interspersed with warehouses and factories that manufactured auto parts, stored steel, or stocked heavy machinery.

With the blessings of Hinky Dink Kenna and Bathhouse John Coughlin, John Torrio started to build alliances with other gangs and ward heelers throughout this surging, ruthless city. Instead of throwing down the gauntlet and issuing challenges to turf, Torrio and his city hall puppets viewed the city's liquor and vice trade as a pie to be sliced and shared. As Capone stood by his boss and quietly watched him work, the young bodyguard saw how a variety of ethnic and territorial rivalries were negotiated into partnerships that avoided conflict.

"He was just one of Johnny Torrio's gunsels when I first met him," recalled Jack Woodford, then a fast-talking law student who worked his way through school playing piano at Colosimo's and other joints in the Levee. "Looking quiet and thoughtful, sitting by himself . . . he had the eyes and look and build of a wounded water buffalo as he sat there, leaning over the table, one hand resting on his opposite forearm."

Content to be in Torrio's shadow, Capone remained shy and observant as his boss added a twist to plans for organizing the

Jack "Greasy Thumb" Guzik, financial mastermind of Torrio and Capone's empire.

underworld: Recognizing that the Levee could still serve as a base of his operation, Torrio offered other gangsters a chance to share the out-of-town bounty in Burnham and other suburbs. He started with the Jews, cutting a deal with Jack "Greasy Thumb" Guzik. Born in Moscow and one of eight children who arrived with their parents, Max and Mamie, in 1892, Guzik learned the vice trade from his father, who parlayed a cigar maker's wages into a career as a precinct captain for Hinky Dink and Bathhouse John. Though he would serve eight months for a 1917 vice conviction, Greasy Thumb used his accounting and bookkeeping skills to work his way into the upper echelons of the city's rackets. By 1921 he exercised control over city patronage workers, west side police precincts, trucking routes, dice games, and bordellos. Like Little John, Greasy Thumb excelled at the details. After a day of reviewing the splits, and calculating the layoff and the drop, he returned to his wife, Rose Lipschitz, and their three children, in an affluent suburb of the city.

At first Torrio proposed a partnership in a brewery, which Guzik immediately accepted. On top of controlling retail distribution for his west side network, Guzik could step into wholesale and production, owning a piece of the barrel, keg, and glass of bootleg beer. As business boomed, Torrio and Guzik expanded, collaborating on The Roamer Inn, a roadhouse in the working-class suburb of Posen. This combination of tavern, jazz joint, dance hall, and whorehouse attracted the growing number of workers who could afford a few hours of pleasure between shifts. The front-room bar and restaurant jumped to music and the jingle of slot machines, while the back offered a stark contrast—a bare room lined with benches.

"The girls we knew were really on the dogwatch," remembered Chicagoland bassist Muzz Mezzrow in his memoir *Really the Blues*. "They paraded around in teddies or gingham baby rompers with big bows in the back, high-heeled shoes, pretty silk hair ribbons twice as big as their heads and rouge an inch thick all over their kissers. When a john had eyeballed the parade and made his choice, he would follow her upstairs, where the landlady sat at a little desk in the hall. This landlady would hand out a metal check and a towel to the girl, while the customer forked over two bucks. Then the girl was assigned a room number. All night long you could hear the landlady calling out in a bored voice, like a combination strawboss and timekeeper, 'All right Number Eight, all right Number Ten—somebody's waiting. Don't take all night.' She ran that joint with a stopwatch.''

To prepare Capone for more responsibilities, Little John occasionally assigned him to work with Greasy Thumb, who feared that his plump stature made him an easy target for shakedowns and Black Hand extortionists. An assailant might think twice if Greasy Thumb had Al at his side. Torrio remained his mentor and idol, continuing to serve as a distant but caring father who directed Capone's future; Guzik, however, offered the hands-on guidance of an older brother, frequently bringing him home and sharing family life. To further Capone's education, Torrio and Guzik dispatched their protégé into the netherworld of prostitution. While they worked to form an alliance with the Irish gang led by north side hooligan Dion "Babyface" O'Banion, Al started at the bottom, managing a discount whorehouse—the first step toward a position of real authority. Recounting his visit to "an old brick, two story building, weather beaten and unpainted," writer Irle Waller described the young Capone as a broad-shouldered man standing at the cathouse entrance "with part of a hairy chest" exposed.

With every hope of eventually doing business with the Sicilians clustered around the Genna brothers of Taylor Avenue—and the back of the stockyards Germans and Irish organized by Frank Ragen's Colts and the four O'Donnell brothers—Torrio and Guzik focused on the north side districts controlled by O'Banion. "Chicago's arch criminal," Police Chief Morgan Collins said of Babyface O'Banion, "who has killed or at least seen to the killing of at least 25 men."

To forge an alliance with O'Banion, Torrio proposed that they share an interest in the Sieben brewery located in the heart of O'Banion's north side turf. Torrio was facing an endless demand for high-quality beer, and he needed the equipment, labor, and storage capacity to have a solid local supply. If he provided cash and distribution, then O'Banion could match the contribution with protection and other services that would allow a round-the-clock operation. While each group was suspicious of the other, they came to terms: Torrio made the initial outlay of cash, O'Banion provided the muscle.

From his vantage point, Capone overheard a snippet of conversation that showed how Torrio had turned a potential rivalry into a vast windfall. As Torrio and Guzik reviewed the books for the brewery deal, they saw that their organization would take in $4 million worth of beer sales for 1921.

✦ ✦ ✦

"... utterly reliable and unquestioningly loyal."

Al started 1922 with a promotion: He left the back alley cathouses and joined Torrio at his new headquarters, a four-story commercial building located down the block from the gaudy scene at Colosimo's. At first Torrio used the modest, red-brick building at 2222 South Wabash as an unsuspected and little-known haven for many of his low-level employees and their fellow travelers. On the ground floor, he built a bar, and placed a few tables and booths that masked the solid steel door to his offices. On the second and third floors, he gave his boys a chance to bet on horses, throw dice, and play cards, serving as the bank that occasionally allowed a player to draw an advance against his wages. The fourth floor offered a fresh supply of women. As word of the Wabash Avenue spot began to spread to all the important members of Chicago's gangland syndicates, they proffered the sobriquet that became infamous: "the Four Deuces."

With his headquarters becoming a popular attraction, Torrio needed protection, so he summoned Al, whose first task was to plant himself on the sidewalk, survey for a possible attack, and then angle a few passing marks for a quick score. "I saw him there a dozen times, coat collar turned up, hands deep in his pockets," recalled reporter Courtney Ryley Cooper. "He fell in step with a passerby and mumbled, 'Got some nice-looking girls inside.'"

As the saloon's notoriety grew, Torrio turned to Capone to help manage its operations and then gave him a new assignment in the basement of the Four Deuces. Working out of a walled-in anteroom sometimes referred to as the Vault (and that would later become the subject of a Geraldo Rivera television show), Capone and others drew the task of hunting down disloyal hoods and administering punishment.

According to the Cook County circuit court judge John H. Lyle, a glad-handing pol and jurist who alternated the roles of self-appointed crusader against, and self-designated chronicler of, gangland, the cellar was the scene of repeated torturings, beatings, and killings. Torrio relied on Capone's muscle to break down his competition or scare off rivals, Lyle said, and other hoods began to talk about the basement. "I got some firsthand information about the resort from [Levee pimp and whoremaster] Mike 'de Pike' Heitler, who bitterly resented the mob's invasion into his field," Lyle wrote in his memoirs, *The Dry and Lawless Years*. "Shuffling into my chambers one afternoon, he told me: 'They snatch guys they want information from and take them to the cellar. They're tortured until they talk. Then, they're rubbed out. The bodies are hauled through a tunnel into a trap door opening in the back of the building. Capone and his boys put the bodies in cars and then they're dumped out on a country road, or maybe in a clay hole or rock quarry.'"

Intimidated by tales that emerged from the crypt beneath the Four Deuces, many gangsters were willing to give Torrio a chance to work out his citywide plans: The first step required Torrio to rent the Sieben brewery and produce beer inside the city limits. This move immediately cut the cost of transport, and the lower price made his brew a best-seller. With beer sales creating a vast pool of cash, Torrio and Guzik approached the owners of the Gambrinus, Standard, George Hoffman, Pfeiffer, West Hammond, Best, Manhattan, and Stege breweries. After the deals were closed, Torrio operated more than $5 million worth of physical assets and Guzik had amassed a working capital fund of more than $20 million. Arranging for the protection to operate these properties, Torrio methodically acquired his competition, positioning himself as a sole source at a price of $50 per barrel.

To supply hard liquor and rum, Torrio agreed to a deal that

The Vault, scene of Capone's early thuggery.

allowed Babyface O'Banion and his north side Irish to control the imports that came out of Windsor, Ontario, wheeled through Detroit, and rolled across Michigan and Indiana. Once it was delivered to the gang's warehouse off Chicago's Clark Street, O'Banion and his lieutenants, George "Bugs" Moran, Vincent "Schemer" Drucci, and Earl Wajciechowski (a.k.a. Hymie Weiss) cut the booze for local distribution. On the city's south side, Torrio had a similar arrangement with the six Genna brothers, who ran a series of home stills, or "alky cookers," in the Little Italy section along Taylor Street. By letting the Gennas distribute and sell the gut-wrenching snorts of moonshine, Torrio won permission to garage his delivery trucks in their neighborhood, a crucial crossroads for citywide traffic.

With his beer network operating at full blast by June 1922, Torrio rewarded Al with an ownership share of the Four Deuces: On top of his salary, Capone began to draw up to twenty-five percent of the weekly profits generated by the underworld's most infamous saloon. For the first time in his life, Capone was an owner instead of a worker.

Showing that he had diligently learned his lessons, Al immediately printed business cards that offered him the veneer of legitimacy as a secondhand furniture dealer. He rented the storefront immediately to the north of the Four Deuces, stenciled the name Alphonse Capone on the window, and stocked the room with a few tables and dressers, chairs and chests. To complete the deception, the newly established hood arranged for a badge and an identification card that placed him as a special deputy employed by the Cook County sheriff.

"This was an indulgence easily bought," Woodford recalled, and it legalized the .22-caliber pistol that Al packed in the right pocket of his overcoat.

, With his gun and badge, Capone had finally arrived as a

person deserving of attention in Chicago's underworld. He had earned his reputation as Torrio's muscle, learned from him and Guzik, and had found himself an observer to many of the deals that shaped the city's life. "Johnny came to know that Al was utterly reliable and unquestioningly loyal," Woodford remembered.

Torrio's respect and trust were essential to Capone's success. Within six months, the young hood had leapfrogged from an income of several hundred dollars a month to several thousand. Though Al remained gregarious, he hid this side of his personality to win favor with Little John, who continued to adhere to his patrician ways. While other gangsters enjoyed flashy parties, Al resisted any display of his lust for the jazz life, aware that his rise in the ranks depended on his ability to complement—not overshadow—Little John. Despite his appetites for dancing in jazz joints and whoring in out-of-the-way roadhouses, young Al presented himself to Little John as a willing and worthy disciple ready to bring his family to Chicago. The first relative to arrive was Ralph, who easily returned to Torrio's employment. With his brother settled into an underworld job, Al made arrangements for wives, children, siblings, and mother.

Flush with the success of bootleg dollars, Capone openly shopped for a house in the sleepy south side, where new brick bungalows and duplexes sprouted for the workingmen and women who climbed their way into steady jobs at factories, the stockyards, steel mills, or the downtown office corridors. In his own name, Capone purchased a two-story dwelling at 7244 Prairie Avenue. Within weeks, the entire Capone clan, except Ralph, moved in.

The only Italian family on a block of thirty-four houses that sheltered Americans of Scottish, Irish, and German descent, the Capones embraced the neighborhood, with Mae or Teresina engaging other women in stories about recipes and child rearing. Al invited neighbors to sample the family's spicy spaghetti sauces and other homemade delights. Five-year-old Sonny was seen throwing a ball with his father; Al's sister, fourteen-year-old Mafalda, rode her bicycle around the block. Though the Capones were Catholic and Teresina immediately began to attend mass at St. Columbanus, the family made fast friends with a Presbyterian minister who lived two doors away.

The fifteen-room Capone house quickly took on the opulent furnishings of gangland: The upstairs den featured floor-to-ceiling mirrors and gilded trim; a seven-foot bathtub added to the luxury of marble sinks. Reinforced concrete thickened the walls, and steel bars were fashioned into window grates. A garage for two cars and a widened driveway dominated the narrow yard, leaving room for only one tree. While the front of the house contained a small door that opened to a second-story veranda, the back featured a steel gate designed to project the image of a fortress.

Like the Brooklyn teen who had repeatedly used his wits and guile to straddle the world of his father's humble home and the high-stepping hustles of Sands Street or Coney Island, the newly established Chicago gangster bounced back and forth from the quiet of his Prairie Avenue home to gaudy nights of drinking, gambling, and whoring in nightclubs and speakeasies that bought beer from the Torrio organization.

Despite his caution, Capone made a mistake during one night of adventure in August 1922. Stepping out of the Four Deuces and climbing behind the wheel of a deluxe sedan registered to one of Torrio's legitimate holding companies, Capone was joined by a woman in the front seat and three men in the rear. They turned north on Wabash, raced out of the Levee, and streaked past the knot of rail spurs and warehouses that criss-crossed the corners between 18th and 12th streets. At the southern edge of the loop, Capone pressed on, rolling between the skyscrapers and driving above the Illinois Central tracks that tucked under the asphalt and came to a stop at the Randolph Street platforms. As his car approached the station's entrance, he yanked a hard right, unaware that cabbie Fred Krause sat in his parked taxi hoping to pick up a fare. When Capone's roadster rear-ended the cab, Krause was thrown from his seat, ending up on the sidewalk.

According to an account circulated to the newspapers by the City News Bureau—a local wire service that still covers police matters for Chicago's dailies and radio stations—the accident occurred when "Alfred Caponi . . . [of] the Four Deuces, a notorious house of public disorder at 2222 South Wabash . . . crashed into a town taxicab driven by Fred Krause, 741 Drake Avenue, at North Wabash Avenue and East Randolph Street, injuring the driver. Three men and a woman, who were with Caponi, fled before the arrival of the police."

Though reporters did not know of him and his importance to the underworld, the police brass understood whom they had nabbed and charged with felony counts of driving while intoxicated, carrying a concealed weapon, and assault with a motor vehicle. As crooked superiors realized that one of their biggest patrons had mistakenly been shown the indignities of a lockup, detectives and sergeants worked on misplacing the paperwork needed for a hearing in criminal court.

Within a few hours, the charges were dropped.

For months the plans brokered by Torrio prevailed, and Chicago remained awash in beer and liquor. With Mayor Big Bill Thompson's city hall firmly devoted to gangsters and policemen openly for sale, the rackets prospered as municipal finances turned from producing a regular surplus to a deficit that accumulated to $4 million. In the face of repeated abuses and widespread graft, Big Bill continued his tirades against King George and barnstormed in his open touring car, clinging to the belief that his hotheaded anti-Prohibition oratory might beat back the growing outcry for reform. By the beginning of 1923, one reporter had dubbed him "the bad breath of Chicago politics."

❧ ❧ ❧

"To hell with the public."

Adding to the stench was a series of scandals that climaxed in the indictment of his campaign manager, Fred Lundin. With Big Bill playing Hizzoner and crony Len Small as governor, Lundin, now a congressman, enjoyed unbridled access to city hall's patronage and its largesse. Chicagoans had long become accustomed to dirty dealings, but their tolerance was tested by Lundin's alleged plunder from the city's school board. As 1923 began, prosecutors indicted Lundin and twenty-three coconspirators in a scheme to steal more than $1 million by overpaying for textbooks and school supplies. The prosecution painted Lundin as a pol so greedy that he would steal from children. One witness told investigators that Lundin shamelessly scoffed at any attempt to limit the graft. "To hell with the public," Lundin was reported as saying, "we're at the trough now and we're going to feed."

Clarence Darrow and his partner Charles Erbstein masterminded the defense of the fallen public officials and kept them out of jail. But the public airing of these charges inflicted enormous political damage on Thompson and galvanized the forces of reform. Democrats turned to a judge of impeccable credentials, William "Decent" Dever, whose well-organized, methodical challenge forced Thompson to backpedal. Though Torrio wanted his gangsters to keep a low profile and quietly tend to the business of shipping suds and booze, his alliance with the city began to break down.

In early 1923, as Dever's surging popularity prompted Thompson to withdraw from the race, Torrio's citywide network of beer runners and bootleggers started to unravel. When Irish gangsters led by Spike, Walter, and Tommy O'Donnell claimed they were shortchanged by "Polack Joe" Saltis and his allies in the neighborhood behind the sprawling stockyards, corner-to-corner rumbles and truck hijackings interrupted a series of deliveries and lucrative cash collections. Within a few weeks, the O'Donnells carved out their own turf, created their own brew, and began selling it below Torrio's price of $50 per barrel.

While most of the city focused on the fall of Thompson and on Dever's mayoral vows to end the beer wars, Torrio gave Capone his first big assignment as a gang leader—to create and execute a plan that would smash the O'Donnells' renegade operation. Showing his guile and tactical bravado, Al crafted a plan of attack that simultaneously defeated the insurgents and captured the public's attention.

On September 7, 1923, George "Sport" Bucher, George Meeghan, an ex-con named Jerry O'Connor, and Steve, Walter, and Tommy O'Donnell tried to shake down a speakeasy run by Jacob Geis at 2154 West 51st Street. Because Geis refused to buy the O'Donnell beer and preferred to keep Torrio as his supplier, the hoods smashed his skull and rained similar blows upon bartender Nick Gorysko. Instead of calling it a night, the O'Donnells began a sweep of five other Torrio speakeasies.

In their bloodlust, they did not realize that Capone had arranged for three goons to follow them. With Danny McFall— a member of the Ragen Social Club—leading the counterattack, the showdown occurred at Joe Klepka's bar on South Lincoln Street. As Spike O'Donnell joined his brothers in raiding this bar, McFall burst in and fired shots that cleared the floor except for O'Connor. To keep everyone at bay, McFall seized O'Connor and held him at gunpoint. According to witnesses, another Capone triggerman, Frank McErlane, walked through the doors, pulled out a sawed-off shotgun, and took O'Connor to the sidewalk. A moment later, McErlane blew off O'Connor's head.

The newspapers feasted on the latest eruption of Chicago's beer battles—reporters finally learning of the man whose name they once misspelled. Though Capone kept clear of the crime scenes, cops and scribes had begun to hear whispers of his involvement. Unlike Torrio, the young Capone enjoyed his emerging notoriety. With Torrio's blessing, he was encouraged to present himself as a man who would not think twice about murder or violence. Now worried that the latest rounds of competition would set off a protracted war for control of his beer empire, Torrio wanted Capone to be known as a notorious enforcer, a role that Capone relished.

Ten days after O'Connor's killing, reporters were once again treated to a gruesome beer war hit. When the O'Donnells' drivers tried to run through a makeshift blockade south of Chicago, a volley of gunfire erupted. Though the trucks would eventually move on, Meeghan and Bucher were discovered the next morning—their arms tied behind their backs, their faces torn open by buckshot. An hour after the bodies were found, newly elected Mayor Dever summoned his police chief, Morgan Collins, for a session with reporters. "Collins, there's a dry law on the nation's books," Dever thundered. "This town will immediately become dry. Tell your captains, I will break every police official in whose district I hear of a drop of liquor being sold."

Though the announcement made great copy for headline writers and gave reporters another chance to snoop around Capone, it also sent a clear message to Torrio. Recognizing that he would have to simultaneously fight city hall and rival gangsters, Torrio used a politician to offer Morgan Collins $100,000 per month if the cops halted the attacks that included raids on private homes stocking bottles of liquor. In response, the police chief ordered his detectives to padlock the Four Deuces.

The saloon quickly reopened, but Torrio saw that protection could not be bought and he turned to his alternative—a new headquarters where a friendly mayor, police chief, and bureaucrats could provide the stability needed to operate bootlegging, gambling, and sex businesses. Though Torrio and Greasy Thumb Guzik had already infiltrated a number of distant suburbs, from Burnham in the southeast to Elgin in the northwest, Torrio turned to Cicero, a working-class town due west of the city, organized around the massive Western Electric factory. Within weeks, Torrio forced a deal with Cicero's political boss Eddie Vogel that allowed him to sell beer anywhere in town. With Al's muscle men holding the upper hand on the streets and Guzik controlling the books, Torrio felt he could leave the country for a few months and resettle his mother in Italy.

His departure led to an escalation of the beer wars, and Capone received his first opportunity to respond without his boss looking over his shoulder. Unwilling to abide by the agreement, the south side O'Donnells once again roughed up saloonkeepers loyal to Torrio, McErlane, and Saltis. Instead of a barroom shootout or gangland showdown, McErlane and a companion believed to be Walter Stevens ambushed a convoy led by O'Donnell wheelmen William "Shorty" Egan and Morrie Keane, killing Keane and wounding Egan.

Though Egan's survival led to the arrest of McErlane and Danny McFall on three different murder indictments, the charges were quickly dropped. When police asked the O'Donnells to identify the assailants, most of the brothers remained silent. Only Spike showed his frustration, telling the cops, "I can whip this bird Capone with bare fists any time he wants to step out in the open and fight like a man."

Picking up on Spike's tip and other bits of underworld gossip, the police questioned Capone, who easily danced away. "Whenever Al was wanted, he would brazenly march into police headquarters at 11th Street and State," Woodford recalled, "and he would always walk out."

Shortly after the cops quizzed Capone, Walter O'Donnell was gunned down. The underworld knew that Capone had struck.

The young Al Capone

CHAPTER THREE

THE RISE

———◆———

Establishing his reputation outside of Torrio's shadow, Capone spearheaded the move to Cicero, choosing a restaurant in a two-story, brown brick building as his headquarters. Owned by Theodore "The Greek" Anton, the Hawthorn Inn at 4833 West 22nd Street was quickly converted into a fortress for what Capone and others believed would be a lengthy stretch of gang warfare. In Cicero, Capone's display of firepower created a safety zone from the cops and from intimidating political boss Eddie Vogel and his puppet Joseph Klenha, the suburb's president who officially controlled local government. Already scared, these men were cheaply purchased with regular envelopes of cash. In return, they allowed Capone's brother Ralph to open the Cotton Club of Cicero, a jazz and gambling joint located four blocks west of the Hawthorn Inn.

The Cotton Club gained notoriety as a spot for many of the city's best musicians, allowing them to break down the color line.

Bix Beiderbecke, the young Louis Armstrong, Kid Oliver, Earl Hines were called on to entertain. According to bass player Milt Hinton—a south side musician who doubled as one of Capone's bootleggers to black districts—the Cotton Club's house band gave "all my peers a chance" to earn $75 per week. Though Hinton described Ralph as "really mean," he lavished praise on Al as the only white gangster in Chicago who gave black musicians a fair shake. "Capone had the whole thing covered," Hinton wrote in his memoirs, *Bass Line*.

With Bottles settled, Al brought his brother Frank into the front end of the vice trade. Relying on the twenty-nine-year-old's tall, dark-haired good looks, Al employed Frank as the organization's emissary to Cicero's city hall, local merchants, and bankers. Besides keeping merchants and pols in line, Frank was the trusted liaison to various real estate and financial interests at the Pinkert State Bank, where the organization made cash deposits that ran into the millions.

Capone quickly saw how the relocation to Cicero paid off: Within months, the organization had kept control of its Chicago operation and eluded Dever's attacks. At the same time, Frank had spread enough payola to ensure that Klenha and his compliant slate of Republicans would run unopposed in Cicero's elections, scheduled for April 1, 1924. Everything appeared to be in place, except for the local newspaper, the *Cicero Tribune*. Instead of filling its pages with fluffy features on church socials or the customs of residents who honored their Bohemian heritage, the weekly of 10,000 copies dedicated itself to hard-boiled coverage of local politics. Under the guidance of its owner-editor, Robert St. John, the *Cicero Tribune* refused to ignore Al Capone's wholesale purchase of local government.

The son of a pharmacist from nearby Oak Park, the broad-shouldered St. John brought to his job a youthful passion that matched Capone's ambition. The twenty-five-year-old journalist had the energy, drive, stamina, and moral conviction to chase the stories of gangster influence and publish them. Fueled by his outrage at crooks corrupting this quiet, working-class town, St. John understood that the Czech and Bohemian immigrants wanted beer but had no intention of surrendering their streets to hoods.

What was once seen as no contest became a contentious race between Rudolph Hurt and Klenha. With access to St. John's front page and the news sections of Chicago's seven dailies, Hurt hammered away, gaining support.

Without Torrio to exercise restraint and figure out a mediated settlement between the factions battling for Cicero, Al Capone relied on his instincts as a brawler. He struck first: On the night before the election, March 31, 1924, goons mugged the Democratic candidate for town clerk, William Pflaum, wrecking his office. As the polls opened at 6 A.M. on the morning of April 1, thugs cruised the streets in black sedans, jumping out to harass voters and even candidates.

By midmorning, one of Cicero's leading reformers, Cook County judge Edmund Jarecki, believed that the only way to protect his hometown and its residents was an armed invasion by Chicago police. The Chicago police could not enter Cicero without a court order, but in a hastily arranged proceeding that included Dever and Police Chief Morgan Collins, seventy of Chicago's patrolmen, five squads of detectives, and nine squads of motorized police were deputized for the official purpose of protecting the shift of 20,000 Western Electric workers as they left their jobs.

Jarecki, Dever, and other city hall reformers did not see that their best intentions would inadvertently lead to a series of deadly misunderstandings. First, uniformed cops were quickly dispatched to the suburban streets; then, plainclothes detectives assembled at the Lawndale station house, the precinct closest to the border between Chicago and Cicero. As the brass organized a column of unmarked cars, known as flivvers, they also issued shotguns to these officers. When the flivver squads pulled out of the station and drove west in a single file, the unmarked police column was mistaken for a patrol of heavily armed hoods.

Positioned near the Western Electric plant—which sat near the line demarking Cicero from Chicago—St. John saw the caravan approach and cross the border at a speed of forty-five to fifty miles per hour. At the same time, witnesses would later testify, a neatly dressed Frank Capone had stepped onto the sidewalk, exiting a building that he was trying to lease by legitimate means. As Frank innocently strode to the corner, the driver of the first flivver squad recognized him and immediately screeched to a halt. Behind the lead car, sedans blocked off the street. Frank Capone suddenly turned. Believing he was cornered by a throng of rival hoods, he went for his right pocket. His hand barely made it. The policemen opened fire, pumping their shotguns until he fell; then they started anew.

The killing of Frank only escalated the level of thuggery. As Al and Ralph Capone went to the Cicero morgue to identify their brother's corpse—which news photographers had already snapped on the slab—hoods blackjacked a policeman, and two men were gunned down near the Hawthorn Inn. Despite the bloodshed and violence, voters continued to come to the polls, making the race extremely tight. When the ballots were counted, Capone's slate led by Klenha prevailed by a margin of 7,878 votes to 6,993.

Frank Capone's funeral gave the public its first real clue about the beginning of a new era in Chicago's underworld.

⤜ CICERO ⤛

With Mayor William "Decent" Dever determined to launch raid after raid on speakeasy, brewery, gaming house, and bordello, John Torrio assigned his handpicked henchman, Al Capone, to scout a location for a safe headquarters beyond the reach of Chicago's police. Though Torrio's club, the Four Deuces, could remain as the organization's outpost in the Levee, he instructed Capone to consider a site that could handle all of the gang's needs—for an office, hideaway, meeting rooms, food, and easy access to the city's streets.

In 1923 Capone showed his tactical acumen: He methodically worked his way through the western suburbs until he came across the quiet, sleepy grid of Cicero, where 60,000 people lived in neat bungalows and courtyard apartment buildings. Mostly Bohemian immigrants and their descendants, these men and women were solid working-class citizens employed at the nearby Western Electric plant or the rows of warehouses and rail yards that checkerboarded the industrial neighborhoods of south Chicago.

Near the end of that year, Torrio and Capone made their first move into Cicero, relocating a brothel from the Levee there. At first Cicero's political boss, Eddie Vogel, ordered his cops to close the joint. When Little John Torrio tried again and received the same result, he ordered Capone to raid one of Vogel's speakeasies and destroy all the slot machines. The tit-for-tat strategy worked, prompting a meeting in which Torrio quietly made his point: Capone would open the gang's headquarters and Vogel would be allowed to keep his political clout provided he followed orders. If Vogel challenged Capone's authority, then Cicero would be torn apart.

In exchange for bribes that totaled thousands upon thousands of dollars, Vogel delivered the loyalty of the town's elected officials.

"The Capones owned the whole town, from the street corner to every desk at city hall and the police station," crusading editor Robert St. John would later say. "It was an invasion and they just took over while Mayor Dever made it unsafe for the gang to be in Chicago. Once they bought the election for 'Big Bill' Thompson to return to Chicago's mayoralty in 1927, the Capones left as if nothing happened.

"To them, it was just here today and gone tomorrow. Business as usual. To the town, it was a nightmare that still lasts."

Mourners lined up for more than two blocks, giving this quiet strip of Prairie Avenue a rude awakening to the identity of its only family of Italian heritage. "Gangland Bows At Slain Chief's Bier," announced the *Chicago Daily News*, which reported that more than 3,000 roses decorated the inside of the Capone house. When the wake ended, a procession of 100 cars knotted traffic from the blossom-bedecked residence to Mt. Olivet Cemetery.

❖ ❖ ❖

"Gunman Killed By Gunman"

In covering the largest spectacle since Big Jim Colosimo's death, the *Tribune* was the first to publicize Frank's brother as "Scarface," but its reporters still bungled his proper name, calling him "Alfred" or "Toni." Though some scribes had known him and traded a few words before Frank's killing, Al Capone remained a mystery. The Chicago dailies were aware of his association with Torrio and his connection to the Four Deuces; St. John exposed Al's relocation to Cicero; and the cops suspected him in a couple of murders but couldn't even stick him with a few felonies for drunk driving and assault. The pieces didn't add up. Gangsters turned out for his brother's funeral as if royalty had passed away. But no one could get a bead on him.

While Capone's impulse dictated a counterattack and a public accounting for his brother's death, Greasy Thumb Guzik counseled patience and restraint. In the absence of Torrio and his tactical abilities, the financial whiz served as the voice of moderation. Besides explaining the disadvantages of a gang assault on cops, Guzik appealed to Capone's sense of family: One brother dead and another hunted by police would hurt the Capones more than help them.

To the relief of Guzik and others in the gang, Al relented. By the time Torrio came back from Italy, Capone had made sure that his gains were secure in Cicero; he had solidified his alliances with Polack Joe Saltis, the Genna Brothers, and others. Following Little John's suggestion, Capone took the unusual step of formally appearing at the coroner's inquest and testifying as the grief-stricken brother. But after the coroner ruled for the police, Capone expressed his outrage to the papers and returned to the underworld.

A month after the shooting, Torrio, Guzik, and Capone started to reap the profits generated by their complete ownership of Cicero's political machinery: On May 1, their organization opened Chicago's largest booze, dice, and sex operations on the streets surrounding the Hawthorn Inn. Loosely known as the Ship, this combination speakeasy, gaming parlor, and whorehouse catered to virtually every form of vice and contraband. With the Ship setting sail, the organization also opened scores of other speakeasies, gaming joints, and cribs around Cicero. As John Kobler pointed out in his chronicles of Prohibition, within the first week the horse races alone brought in an average of $50,000 per day.

Surprised by the enormous volume of bets, Torrio, Guzik, and Capone struck a deal designed to ease the heat on local pols: Police raids would be permitted if advance warning was given. These forays would offer city officials the charade of playing straight, and the hoods also agreed to limit the number of prostitutes and cathouses operating in Cicero. This pledge caused them to open bordellos in nearby suburbs. In exchange, the organization demanded a complete monopoly.

Klenha and his slate eagerly agreed—as did their Republican party boss Eddie Vogel. Everything was in place except Al Capone. Rattled by the killing of his brother and Torrio's pressure to check his anger, Capone began his evening rounds on the night of May 8 at the Four Deuces, where he settled in with a few hoods. The socializing was interrupted by Guzik, who told Capone that a beer hijacker, "Ragtime" Joe Howard, was down the street talking trash. When Guzik mentioned that he was slapped and called "a dirty little kike" by Howard, Capone jumped to his feet, tightly wound and determined to defend the honor of his partner.

Within minutes, Capone tracked Howard to Hymie Jacobs's saloon at 2300 South Wabash. As Capone walked in, two regular customers, mechanic George Bilton and carpenter David Runelsbeck, were at the bar sipping mugs of beer. Howard stood at the bar talking to Jacobs and another crook, Tony "Mouth" Bagnolia.

Ragtime Joe extended his hand to greet Capone. "Hello, Al," he was heard to say.

Capone didn't waste time. He grabbed Ragtime Joe and demanded an explanation for his treatment of Guzik.

Instead of giving Capone an answer, Howard tried the brush-off. "Listen, you dago pimp," he sneered, "why don't you run along and take care of your broads."

Capone pulled out his revolver and fired all six shots. Four burst through Howard's face; two struck his shoulder on his way down. As the cops and reporters hustled to the scene, Capone fled to Cicero.

During their initial interviews with detectives, "Mouth" Bagnolia kept his shut, but saloonkeeper Jacobs and his patrons Runelsbeck and Bilton gave solid accounts of the shooting. "I am certain it was Capone," said the chief of detectives, Michael

Hughes, who told the *Tribune* that he had issued a general order for the suspect's arrest. The paper hyped its scoop with headlines in seventy-two-point type: "Gunman Killed By Gunman."

As the papers hit the streets and Capone hit his hideaway, Torrio began to work his magic. When detectives returned to interview Bilton, they could not find him. Runelsbeck changed his story and said at the coroner's inquest that he could no longer identify the killer. Jacobs recanted, telling authorities that he had either taken a phone call or ducked into the safe to retrieve a roll of nickels and therefore did not see who pulled the trigger. When the cops arrested Runelsbeck and Jacobs on charges of being accessories to murder, a judge ordered their release.

After a month in hiding, Capone reappeared on June 11, strolling into police headquarters. "I hear the police are looking for me," he told the desk sergeant. "What for?"

Instead of going to the lockup or the interrogation room, the cops escorted Capone directly to the Criminal Courts Building, where a young prosecutor, William McSwiggin, had told reporters that he could shake a confession out of the gangster. The son of police sergeant Anthony McSwiggin—a cop who was seen as a saint by reformers and a sinner by gangsters—the twenty-six-year-old William enjoyed the same two-faced reputation.

Within four hours, Capone was released. When the coroner's inquest held its final session on the matter, the jurors ruled that Howard had died from "bullets fired from a revolver or revolvers in the hand or hands of one or more unknown white male persons."

Though Torrio had worked hard to keep his protégé and partner out of trouble, the killing of Frank Capone and Joe Howard clearly marked a turning point for Chicago's rackets.

The attention of the news media, the coroner's inquest, and the ever-expanding demand for booze, women, and dice snowballed into instability. The arrangements of 1923 had become obsolete—too many crooks wanted too much of the growing profits from brew. With Mayor Dever's police eager to make any arrest, rival gangsters understood that betrayal to the cops offered another tactic in their competition for spoils.

While Torrio pondered the possibility of stepping down, the six Genna brothers of Little Italy flexed their muscles: An aggressive gang that did not flinch at the use of violence, the Gennas solidified their hold on the Italian and Sicilian neighborhoods by procuring federal government authorization to produce "industrial alcohol." This legitimate still merely served as a front for a network of tenement alky cookers that supplied the kick for cheap rotgut hooch that could be sold to speakeasies for much less than the whiskey delivered through Babyface O'Banion and his north side crew. At the beginning of Prohibition, Torrio had used his diplomatic skills to broker a deal that satisfied both the Gennas and O'Banion, but now the Gennas poached at O'Banion's turf and claimed that they were merely adding another product without going into direct competition against their rival.

Both sides sought assistance from Torrio and Capone, who positioned themselves beyond the fray. O'Banion made a direct demand for help, but Torrio and Capone balked, openly angering him. Torrio and Capone explained that their beer delivery trucks were housed by the Gennas and that they needed more than O'Banion's slight provocation to move against the Sicilians. But aware that the killings of Frank Capone and Joe Howard had distracted Torrio's gang, O'Banion imposed his own solution. He hijacked one of the Gennas' shipments, corralling more than $30,000 worth of moonshine.

When the Gennas threatened retaliation, Torrio decided to intervene and broker a face-saving deal that would avert bloodshed. Still, relations between Torrio and O'Banion continued to sour. As partners in the Sieben brewery, the two men grew suspicious of each other, certain that their association was about to collapse. O'Banion made the first move by coming to Cicero a few days after Howard's killing. At the Hawthorn Inn, he met with Torrio and Capone, seeking to end his involvement in bootlegging and the Chicago rackets. To the surprise of the other two, O'Banion offered to sell his interest in Sieben and relocate to Colorado, where he could enjoy life on top of a mountain and forget about the underworld.

Torrio and Capone took the bait and agreed to pay $500,000

Dion "Babyface" O'Banion, north side rival of Torrio and Capone.

cash in full. The drop was made before completion of the last aspect of the deal—a May 19 meeting at the brewery, where O'Banion pledged to supervise the last of his beer shipments. In anticipation of that gathering, he had learned that Police Chief Collins planned a raid for the same evening. O'Banion's scheme was to have Torrio arrive shortly before the police. While O'Banion figured he could buy his way out of a minor bootlegging rap, he knew the cops would be thrilled to catch Torrio.

On the night of May 19, the police made their move. With shotguns drawn, they raided the brewery just as O'Banion and Torrio were directing goons to load barrels of beer. In a weak effort to preserve his front, O'Banion took the bust with Torrio and twenty-eight others, who were delivered to federal authorities instead of the central lockup or the Cook County criminal courts. Since he was in the federal system, Torrio had no pull. He had to wait his turn to peel off fifty C-notes and post $5,000 bail.

Little John Torrio's arrest, however, guaranteed O'Banion's early death. Throughout May, June, and July Little John assembled lawyers for the defense of his men and also worked to steer Capone through the Howard inquest. Once the coroner's jury ruled that they could not determine who had killed Ragtime Joe, Little John was ready to seek his revenge on Babyface. He turned to Capone for the particulars.

With Torrio looking over his shoulder, Al made all the right moves. Instead of launching a quick strike that could further upset the frazzled alliance between Torrio and the Gennas, he let O'Banion and his partners Bugs Moran and Hymie Weiss attempt to mollify the Sicilians. But O'Banion only increased the pressure. Having grown up near the north side Sicilian enclave known as Little Hell, O'Banion figured his longtime connections with Unione Sicilione president Mike Merlo would help him overpower the recently arrived Gennas and their moonshine trade. Merlo insisted that any effort to kill O'Banion would be taken as a personal affront.

Unfortunately for O'Banion, though, Merlo was seriously ill and on Saturday, November 8, Merlo keeled over. O'Banion cashed in on his friend's death, billing for more than $100,000 worth of flowers in his flower shop. In the rush of business, O'Banion missed one of the smaller purchases—a $750 order from his sworn enemy Jim Genna. While O'Banion worked at his legitimate business—Schofield's Flower Shop, on a strip of State Street directly across from Holy Name Cathedral— Genna walked in, picked up his order, and cased the joint late Sunday evening, November 9.

On Monday, O'Banion and his porter, William Crutchfield, opened early. Around noon, a blue Jewett sedan pulled to a halt across the street from the store, double-parking near the steps that led to the cathedral. On the corner, Gregory Summers, an eleven-year-old junior traffic officer from Holy Name School, spotted the car and the three men who stepped out.

Hunched over a bunch of chrysanthemums, O'Banion never noticed the car. Nearby, Crutchfield swept the floor and saw the trio enter. O'Banion stopped his work and walked to the front portion of the store. His left hand held the pruning shears; he extended his right hand. "Hello boys," he reportedly began. "You want the Merlo flowers?"

"Mr. O'Banion called for me to close the back room door and I did," Crutchfield explained. "I didn't recognize any of the three men; never saw them before, so far as I recall. I shut the door between the back and front rooms of the shop, figuring that Mr. O'Banion had private business with the men."

Less than a minute later, Crutchfield heard gunfire. When he opened the door, he saw O'Banion lying amid containers of carnations and lilies.

The word buzzed across Chicago: Capone had arrived as the underworld's top henchman.

One day after the funeral, O'Banion lieutenant Louis "Two Gun" Alterie openly spoke of the gang war that eventually established Chicago's international notoriety. "If I knew who killed Deany, I'd shoot it out with the killers before the sun rose in the morning and some of us, maybe all of us, would be laying on slabs some place."

Torrio immediately recognized the threat and made arrangements to leave town. In his absence, he tapped Capone as caretaker of the organization. Suspecting that his rivals' desire for vengeance would soon trigger round after round of violence, Torrio felt that Capone's brawn, not Guzik's brain, would preserve the organization and its enterprises.

Capone stepped into his new role by violating one of his boss's cardinal rules: Instead of keeping quiet, Capone sought the limelight. Al recognized the power of the media to create a persona that was bigger than life. Through the newspapers, he simultaneously projected the image of strength and communicated with people he could not meet.

Faced with the braggadocio of Alterie and the snarling threats of his sidekick Bugs Moran, Capone openly dared his adversaries to strike. When reporters tracked him down and sought his response to the vows of vengeance, Capone held court. "Deany was all right," he told the newsmen, "and he was getting along to begin with better than he had a right to expect. But like everyone else his head got away from his hat."

Capone's lengthy statement was a complete contradiction of what he had told reporters six months earlier—when he claimed to hardly know Torrio or bootleggers. But Al now believed this radical change of tactics was needed to draw out his enemies and force a premature showing of their strength.

This gambit required patience and a dash of good luck. As Capone had intended, O'Banion's avengers struck first. On January 12, two days after Angelo Genna threw himself a wedding party for 3,000 people in the Ashland Auditorium, Moran, Schemer Drucci, and Alterie followed Capone's car to an eatery off the corner of 51st and State streets. When Capone stepped out of his black sedan and strolled toward the door, another car streaked by, blasting gunfire. Instead of a single bang-bang of bullets or the pump-clack of shotgun pellets, the rounds exploded with a rat-tat-tat. The Thompson sub-machine gun, a weapon developed for soldiers storming European-style trenches, had arrived in Chicago's gangland.

Though Moran, Drucci, and Alterie were convinced that the rapid spray of lead would at least wound Capone, their marksmanship failed. While Capone ducked into the restaurant, his chauffeur and bodyguard, Sylvester Barton, took a slug in the back.

A few days later, the north side avengers struck again, kidnapping Barton's replacement, a young hood named Tommy Cuiringione, sometimes known as Rossi. When the wheelman remained loyal to his boss and refused to tell of Capone's whereabouts, his captors bound his wrists and ankles, burned his face with cigarettes, then pumped five bullets into his head. His body was dumped in the park.

Al reckoned that his organization had the muscle and stability to wait it out. While the north siders remained intent on revenge, Capone and Guzik continued to expand their stranglehold on beer, women, and gambling. One estimate of the organization's revenues claimed a gross of $60 million in one year. With so much money on the line, Capone decided it was better to make money and stay alive than risk everything on a street-corner gunfight.

When Torrio returned to Chicago for a January 23 court

appearance in his bootlegging case, he continued to counsel restraint, believing that Moran, Drucci, and Alterie would alienate other gangsters and dry up their sources of liquor, thereby cutting their abilities to earn. A day after the pro forma legal proceeding, Torrio and his wife, Ann, enjoyed an unusually mild day, taking in a downtown stroll before going home in a car driven by Sylvester Barton's brother Robert. As they climbed out of the sedan and walked toward their apartment building, 7011 Clyde in South Shore, a blue Cadillac rolled around the opposite corner. Hymie Weiss and Bugs Moran jumped out. First they shot Barton, then took aim at Torrio, firing repeatedly. Two bullets hit him in the neck and chest.

He fell to the street as Weiss and Moran rushed over to shoot again. The next bullet went into his right arm—and then they shot him in the groin. Torrio remained conscious.

To finish the job, Moran put his revolver beside Torrio's temple. A passing laundry truck bought Torrio an extra moment before Moran drew a final bead and pulled the trigger.

Click.

The gun misfired. The hoods fled, leaving Torrio's blood to swirl in a patch of melting ice.

His wife called an ambulance, which rushed to the scene and transported Little John to Jackson Park Hospital, where reporters, hoods, cops, doctors, and nurses congregated around the emergency room.

William "Shoes" Schoemaker, newly appointed chief of detectives, put the case together. Finding a seventeen-year-old janitor, Peter Vessaert, who witnessed the assassination attempt, Schoemaker presented the young man with mug shots and then a lineup. In each instance, Vessaert identified Bugs Moran as one of the assailants. Within a day, Schoemaker

George "Bugs" Moran, O'Banion's partner.

brought Vessaert face-to-face with Moran. "You're the man," said the teenager.

"You're nuts," replied Moran.

"I saw you shoot that man," Vessaert repeated. The police booked Moran, but prosecutor John Sbarbaro and Judge William Lindsay agreed the case was weak. Moran posted $5,000 bail and the charges were dropped.

Recognizing that his wounds had effectively ended his career as the day-to-day overlord of Chicago's rackets, Torrio had one last surprise to offer: Sixteen days after the shooting, he was released from the hospital to appear in U.S. District judge Adam Cliffe's courtroom. Still bandaged and frail, Little John mustered enough strength to stand before the magistrate and enter a guilty plea to a single count of operating a brewery. In exchange for his plea, Cliffe sentenced Torrio to nine months and a $5,000 fine.

Al Capone now became the most feared gangster in Chicago.

While Capone knew how to fight in the streets, he had to learn how to organize a gang. The first need was to keep track of the enormous amount of cash coming in from beer, liquor, gambling, and women. For this task, Capone relied on Guzik, "the only friend I can trust." With Greasy Thumb serving as his right hand on the books, Capone next turned to a Sicilian, Frank "the Enforcer" Nitti, to back up his expertise on muscle and terror and also serve as his emissary to the Unione Sicilione.

❖ ❖ ❖

"Sure I got a racket."

If Nitti and Guzik were ministers to the overlord, then Al's brother Ralph served as one of the chief courtiers. Bottles drew the task of overseeing the marketing of beer and liquor to speakeasies, nightclubs, hotels, and eateries throughout Chicago. To make sure the operation remained under close supervision, Ralph enlisted a cousin, Charlie Fischetti, to be in charge of trucking crews. Fischetti was a soft-spoken transplant from New York, and his mild-mannered ways belied his shrewd business acumen and ability to organize drivers who kept dozens and dozens of rigs rolling across the city. With the help of Lawrence "Dago" Mangano, a local teamster who knew every back alley, Fischetti spearheaded the organization's effort to control the trucking business.

While Bottles, Fischetti, and Mangano kept tabs on the streets, Al spun Chicago's citywide gambling network through Cicero, where he was confident that crooked local pols and cops would not launch a raid. As wire rooms and hole-in-the-wall bookies covered the city, Capone located his headquarters

Jack "Machine Gun" McGurn. His trademark was a nickel pressed into his victim's palm.

in the Hawthorn Smoke Shop, where proven ally Frankie Pope kept hourly tabs on the action.

Capone reserved a special spot for two young hoods on the rise. Murray Llewellyn Humphreys, a tall, stately Welshman, made a name for himself as a dashing and elegant stickup artist who was always seen in a fine suit and camel hair overcoat and was dubbed "Murray the Camel." While Humphreys's suave image caught Capone's eye, the raw, brash athleticism of Jack "Machine Gun" McGurn captured his imagination. Born as Vincent DeMora in the Little Italy section of Taylor Street, the broad-shouldered, slim-hipped kid was the son of an alky cooker employed by the Gennas. After the elder DeMora sold some of his liquor to a freelancer, he was gunned down in 1920, leaving his teenage son, who vowed to avenge the murder. When a neighborhood trainer named Emil Thiery offered the teen a chance to earn money by fighting, he agreed and accepted the Irish name Jack McGurn. Despite his bright start as an amateur, the young pugilist could not sustain his skills over six to eight rounds, so he pulled himself out of the ring. To make a living, McGurn hired himself out as muscle. By the middle of 1925, the police had named him as a suspect in twenty-two killings—five allegedly committed as a reprisal for his father. Though he had never been arrested for murder, McGurn left a well-known calling card: a nickel in the hand of his victim, which meant that the deceased's life was not even worth five cents.

On top of his reputation as a boxer and triggerman, McGurn was also known as a playboy, his dashing dark hair parted in the middle and pomaded to the sides. Like Capone, he loved to dance and listen to music, and he rolled through cabarets and nightclubs. With his bulky boss at his side, McGurn's slender grace stood out.

With his gang in place, Capone tightened his grip on the booming beer and vice trade. In Cicero he exercised complete control over Hawthorn Race Track, a move that added tens of thousands to his daily take. To keep the cash moving in the cycle of sin, Capone, his brother Ralph, and Guzik decided to build a new brothel and gaming parlor in Forest View. Though the joint, in a large brick-and-stone structure, carried a small sign reading The Maple Inn, hoods quickly tabbed it as "the Stockade": A series of secret chambers offered hiding places for the sixty prostitutes who worked as regular staff, and at least one room was soundproofed with cork lining and served as a hideaway for gangsters on the run. Other hiding places were carved out for guns, ammunition, liquor supplies, and explosives.

As the Stockade quickly became a legend that netted thousands each week, the Capones boldly opened yet another large-scale bordello. Perched on the southwestern side of Hawthorn Race Track, this nondescript two-story building operated as a factory. While the Stockade sat beyond Cicero's borders and therefore beyond the circulation area of Robert St. John and his anti-Capone crusade in the *Cicero Tribune*, the new whorehouse was quartered in the paper's prime market. When it opened, St. John immediately entered, claiming to be a customer.

Publication of St. John's exposé kindled a rage of anger. Led by the Reverend Henry Hoover of Berwyn, the West Suburban Citizens Association demanded that local mayors and police chiefs shut down Capone's bordellos and gaming dens. When the small-town pols did nothing, the citizens sought relief from Cook County state's attorney Robert Crowe. Nothing happened, so Hoover conducted a raid of his own, leading a band of citizens into the Hawthorn Smoke Shop, where they came face-to-face with Capone.

"This is the last raid you'll ever pull," Capone warned the preacher. On the way out, two of the raiders were beaten by Capone's muscle men.

Hoover refused to go away. According to author John Kobler, the cleric and his committee raised $1,000, which was given to a member of the rival gang controlled by Hymie Weiss, Schemer Drucci, and Bugs Moran. Within days of the drop, the whorehouse described by St. John burned to the ground.

Two days later, St. John approached his office near the corner of 52nd Avenue. On one side, he noticed a policeman reading a newspaper. Down the street, he saw another cop. Then a black sedan wheeled to the curb. Ralph Capone and slugger Peter Pizak jumped out with two others. St. John was on the concrete after the first round of blows; then he saw the blackjack. The cops never moved.

A week later, St. John left the hospital. Stopping at the desk to settle his bill, the editor was told that the account had been paid by a heavyset man whose face featured a scar along the left cheek. That day, St. John went to the Cicero police station and demanded Capone's arrest. Police Chief Theodore Svoboda refused, telling St. John to return on the following morning.

In an empty room on the second floor of the police station, Capone and St. John came face-to-face. As St. John described the encounter, Capone remained jovial and flippant. "Sure I got a racket," Capone said. "So's everybody. Most guys hurt people. I don't hurt nobody. Only them that get in my way."

Capone told St. John that newspapers provide advertising to his businesses, which cannot legitimately purchase pages or placards. Apologizing for the beating, he claimed that he had instructed his men to keep away from reporters, but a drunken Ralph got out of hand. As Capone fingered his wad to cover St. John's expenses, the editor walked out of the room.

Within a week, St. John learned that Capone and his associates had obtained a controlling interest in the *Cicero Tribune* by buying out creditors and other investors. When Capone's bail bondsman, Louis Cowan, entered the newsroom to announce his appointment as publisher, St. John said, "Well, Mr. Publisher, I guess you and your scar-faced friend have won. Say good-bye to him for me."

St. John never returned to Cicero.

The burning of the bordello gave Capone's rivals a chance to open another front. As Hoover and the reformers of Cicero, Berwyn, and Stickney continued to harass the Hawthorn Smoke Shop, the Hawthorn Inn, and other illicit establishments, Bugs Moran, Hymie Weiss and Schemer Drucci decided to strike at Capone by attacking his allies, the Gennas. Ever since the killing of Dion O'Banion, the Gennas had been among Al's strongest supporters. Once Angelo

Genna became president of the Unione Sicilione, Capone was able to use the civic organization as a legitimate front.

On May 25, as Angelo Genna left a downtown meeting with more than $15,000 cash in his pocket, a touring car began to follow his sedan. Aware that he was being hunted, Genna stepped on the gas and a wild chase began. At the corner of Hudson and Ogden streets his car skidded up the curb and crashed into a lamppost. A minute later, three shotgun blasts killed Angelo.

❧ ❧ ❧

"The verdict is a blow to justice."

As the police cast about for evidence against the killers, Capone and his rivals scrambled to have Tony Lombardo fill Genna's vacancy as president of the Unione Sicilione. Believing that they could block Capone's influence, Moran, Drucci, and Weiss backed Samoots Amatuna for the job and offered a large bounty if he betrayed Lombardo and gunmen Albert Anselmi and John Scalise. Pretending to go along, Amatuna arranged for the showdown to take place on the morning of June 13, 1925, at the corner of Congress and Sangamon streets. At 9 A.M., Moran and Drucci were parked in their automobile, ready to jump out and ambush their prey. They never expected that a car would approach from their rear and open fire on them. The shotgun blasts wounded both Moran and Drucci, who managed to shoot back and drive a few blocks before ditching their car. Both men were found bleeding on the Congress Street sidewalk.

As ambulances took Moran and Drucci to the hospital—where they would eventually recover and refuse to name their assailants—Mike Genna, Scalise, and Anselmi raced south on Western Avenue. At 47th Street, they passed a northbound detective car that contained four plainclothes cops. The commanding officer, Michael Conway, recognized Genna at the wheel and ordered a chase. After turning around, the squad car sounded its siren and speeds reached seventy miles per hour. When a lumber truck crept across the intersection of Western and 59th Street, Genna swerved, but lost control; his car smashed into a telephone pole. Apparently unhurt, the three hoods played opossum.

Conway stepped out of his flivver and approached the gangsters. "Why didn't you stop?" Genna and his crew answered with shotgun blasts, killing officers Harold Olson and Charles Walsh. Conway suffered wounds in the chest. The fourth cop, William Sweeney, retreated to his squad car and fired over the hood.

The gunplay in a crowded industrial district triggered dozens of calls to the police. Genna, Anselmi, and Scalise started to run, and Sweeney chased them, revolver in hand. Though Anselmi and Scalise ducked into an alley, Genna turned to face the officer and raised his shotgun. He pulled the trigger but the barrels were empty; he had forgotten to reload. Sweeney took aim and shot Genna in his thigh, the bullet severing the femoral artery. Unwilling to surrender, a fallen Genna dragged himself to a basement window and wiggled through. Sweeney and two other officers found him on the floor, sitting in a pool of his own blood. After an ambulance attendant attempted to adjust stretcher straps, Genna kicked the man with his good leg. "Take that, you son of a bitch," he snarled. He bled to death before reaching the hospital.

UNIONE SICILIONE

Started as a fraternal organization designed to promote Sicilian culture and help immigrants adapt to the new world, the Unione Sicilione quietly slipped into the feuds between gangsters and politicians, Black Hand extortion crews and labor sluggers. The organization had a membership of 15,000 people who were clustered in overcrowded neighborhoods in Chicago, New York, Philadelphia, and Boston. The group's leadership frequently presented itself as a power broker for bootleggers and hijackers as they scrambled to move and store goods, locate warehouses, garage trucks, and manufacture alcohol during Prohibition.

In Chicago, the Unione's president in the early 1920s, Mike Merlo, openly allied himself with Dion "Babyface" O'Banion, who had grown up in the Sicilian neighborhood known as "Little Hell," a six-square-block patch northwest of the city's downtown. Though John Torrio and Al Capone had frequently approached Merlo about ending his allegiance to the Irishman and his gang, Mike repeatedly refused.

Two days after Mike died of cancer, in November 1924, O'Banion was gunned down and the Torrio-Capone gang began its effort to take over the Unione Sicilione. Over the next seven years, a series of bloody shootouts and rubouts would kill four men who became president of the organization. Newspaper writers dubbed these killings "The Wars of Sicilian Succession." Capone ruthlessly fought to maintain control of the Unione, aware that its nationwide network of members and legitimate businesses offered many opportunities to protect his vice operations. As violence engulfed the Unione's leadership, the newspapers began a series of exposés and articles aimed to show that the organization served merely as a front for competing racketeers. To defend the honor of the Sicilian rank and file of hardworking men and women, the group put forth Constantino Vitello, the Chicago-based vice president, who kept his office despite the murder and mayhem surrounding the presidency.

"Our members are honest Americans," he told reporters in 1927. "The constitution of the Unione, strictly enforced, declares that: No man who has a blot on his character may enter and those who are proved to have committed a felonious act while members will be expelled."

Anselmi and Scalise tried to dodge the cops by jumping on a streetcar, but a local store owner noticed the pair and pointed them out. They did not resist when the officers dragged them off. After charging the duo with killing police officers, State's Attorney Robert Crowe vowed "these men will go straight to the gallows."

While Anselmi and Scalise awaited separate trials for the shootings of detectives Olson and Walsh, death came to another Genna brother, Tony. On the morning of July 8, he was scheduled to meet Giuseppe "Il Cavaliere" Nerone on Grand Avenue, near Cutilla's Grocery. As the two men gripped hands, a gunman stepped behind Genna and shot him five times. Before the police had the chance to question Nerone, he was shot while being shaved in a north side barbershop.

Unwilling to face yet another execution in the family, the remaining Gennas went into hiding, and Capone believed that his friend Tony Lombardo could easily assume the Unione Sicilione's presidency. But Amatuna surprised Al and prevailed in an electoral challenge. After taking office, the new leader recognized the need to ingratiate himself with Capone: As one of his first official acts, Amatuna asked all 15,000 members of the organization to raise money for the defense of Anselmi and Scalise in their first trial. Although the campaign netted $50,000, this success was overshadowed by the bombing of Detective Sweeney's house. No one was hurt, but the well-publicized explosion intimidated many who were called to serve on the jury. After three weeks of selecting a panel, the trial began in October. Assistant State's Attorney William McSwiggin could not live up to his reputation as the "hanging prosecutor." Instead of delivering a murder conviction for the killing of Detective Olson, the jury settled on manslaughter. Scalise and Anselmi broke into wide smiles as

Olson's deaf mother used sign language to tell reporters of her reaction. "The verdict is a blow to justice," she said.

Though Judge William Brothers sentenced the killers to fourteen years and prepared to try the duo for the killing of Detective Walsh, the Unione Sicilione once again began a fund-raising campaign. This time, however, Amatuna's effort took on a new twist: On November 13, as he sat for a haircut and shave in a Cicero barbershop, he was shot five times and killed. After the funeral, Capone's hand-picked candidate, Tony Lombardo, was finally named president of the Unione Sicilione. Capone and his organization shifted their attention back to getting people in and out of prison: First, Little John Torrio was released from Lake County jail. An escort of bodyguards picked him up and drove him through Chicago, stopping at Gary, Indiana, where Little John boarded a train for New York. Once reunited with his wife, he never returned to Chicago, but served the organization as an elder statesman from his retirement home near White Plains.

For their next trial of Anselmi and Scalise, Capone's outfit worked its game plan. To get a jury, lawyers needed to interview 247 prospective candidates. The panel acquitted Anselmi and Scalise on all counts pertaining to the killing of Detective Walsh. Though they were sent to Joliet State Penitentiary to begin serving fourteen years for killing Detective Olson, Capone showed the breadth of his political clout when the Illinois Supreme Court reversed that conviction and ordered yet another trial for the triggermen.

The court did not completely clear Anselmi and Scalise, but the hoods knew exactly whom to thank for their freedom. After seven months behind bars, their first stop in Chicago was a visit to Al Capone.

Capone, as he took control of Chicago

CHAPTER FOUR

BLOODY CHICAGO

—————◆—————

T hough he came to power by inheriting Torrio's beer, sex, and gambling operations, the illness of his seven-year-old boy, Sonny, in 1925 provided the perfect ruse for Capone to make a dramatic move to expand his share of the whiskey market. Until November 1924, Babyface O'Banion had supplied the city with spirits from Canada or rum from Puerto Rico or the Bahamas. But O'Banion's execution and the continued hostilities waged by Hymie Weiss, Schemer Drucci, and Bugs Moran offered Capone another possibility.

By December 1925, Capone believed that he could approach his old boss Frankie Yale and cut a deal that would sidestep the whiskey runs sponsored by Moran, Drucci, and Weiss. Capone knew that this trio ran their contraband directly out of Ontario, and he wanted to tap into Yale's trade, which anchored Scottish or Irish booze in New York and ferried it ashore to Brooklyn or

Newark. From warehouses in Red Hook, Coney Island, and his old stomping grounds in Williamsburg, Capone planned to run a convoy of trucks to Chicago, where the demand for imported whiskey continued to soar.

To finalize this arrangement, Capone needed to meet with Yale in New York—and the illness of Sonny Capone provided cover. Throughout his life, the seven-year-old boy had struggled with his hearing, a malady that resulted from a mastoid infection in his left ear. Chicago doctors warned that an operation might result in permanent damage, so Al and Mae Capone took Sonny to Manhattan for treatment. After visiting three surgeons, the Capones settled on a St. Nicholas Place doctor. "I'll give you $100,000 if you pull him through," Capone reportedly told the physician, who refused the lavish fee and completed the procedure. Sonny would live, but his hearing would always be impaired. On Christmas Eve, the Capones left their boy in the hospital and went to Brooklyn, staying with Mae's parents.

With his wife and child visiting relatives, Al had set the stage for his ambitious gambit. The next night, as Capone would later explain, a friend invited him out for a beer to take his mind off things.

The party ended up at the Adonis Social Club, where Al had first learned how to shoot a pistol. A throng of Italian gangsters caroused while a piano player ran through blues numbers and ragtime ditties. Amid the throng of Italian gangsters, an Irish contingent led by Richard "Peg-Leg" Lonergan held court. At first the festive atmosphere drowned out the suspicion and competition between Yale's thugs, known as "Black Handers," and Lonergan's "White Handers." Though Yale and Lonergan jousted for control of Brooklyn's waterfront and its opportunities to transport and stash booze and hijack or smuggle goods, the Italians wanted the party to appear as the first step toward a partnership.

Shortly after Capone's arrival, he took a seat near the middle of the club. After several rounds of bawdy entertainment, club owner "Fury" Argolia positioned himself behind one of Lonergan's men, Aaron Harms. Drawing a meat cleaver, Argolia landed the blade in the middle of Harms's skull. Then the lights went out and the shooting began.

When Patrolman Richard Morano of the Fifth Avenue Station made his rounds on the morning of December 26, he found Harms in the gutter, a hole chopped out of his head. The trail of blood led to the clubhouse. Morano found Lonergan and his sidekick Cornelius "Needles" Ferry lying dead in front of the piano. On the music stand was the score to "Yes Sir That's My Baby."

A short time later, police found a fourth White Hander, James Hart, crawling on the sidewalk a few blocks away from the club. He survived with multiple gunshot wounds.

Though Hart would refuse to name his attackers, the police rounded up the club management and arrested them and four others, including Capone. The police held them without bail on the hope that Hart would change his mind and press charges. The seven suspects spent three days in the Brooklyn House of Detention before Judge Francis McCloskey received word that the only survivor could not and would not testify against the arrestees. On New Year's Eve, McCloskey dismissed the charges against the men arrested in what tabloids now dubbed the "Adonis Club Massacre."

Capone pulled out of New York with his wife and son, confident that Lonergan's bloody demise cleared the way for Frankie Yale's gang to unload, store, and truck large quantities of booze in and out of New York. In early January, Capone's men would make their first run from Chicago to Brooklyn and back again.

❖ ❖ ❖

". . . the only completely corrupt city in America."

The cumulative damage of prolonged gangster feuds had finally humiliated the reform-minded mayor William Dever. As many of his blueblooded supporters lost faith in his administration, they turned to the Chicago Crime Commission, ostensibly a nonpartisan watchdog group dedicated to documenting the corruption of local government. To the dismay of these well-intentioned citizens, even the privately funded crime commission admitted that Dever's reformers were completely outmaneuvered by gangsters. With complete ownership of suburban governments in Cicero, Stickney, and Forest View, Capone and his men had built safe havens that were beyond the reach of the few honest pols surrounding the mayor. At the same time, Capone's organization continued its constant bribery of Chicago cops on the beat, prosecutors, county officials, aldermen, and ward bosses.

"Chicago is unique," said Charles Merriam, a University of Chicago political science professor who doubled as an alderman and reform leader. "It is the only completely corrupt city in America."

Reformers targeted State's Attorney Robert Crowe, hoping to focus public outrage on his inability to prosecute gangsters. He had won his office on the same ticket as Governor Len Small and Mayor Big Bill Thompson in 1919. The bespectacled prosecutor presented a scholarly appearance and had immediately sought to distance himself from the reach of clubhouse politics. A gifted speaker, he used his office to launch a public campaign for more prosecutors and judges allotted to hear criminal cases. By keeping his name in the newspapers as a crusader for more manpower and a bigger budget, Crowe successfully diverted attention from his record. In 1921—the second full year of his first term—Cook County had recorded 2,309 felony convictions. By the end of 1922, the number of felony convictions had dropped to 1,344, even though the number of major crimes reported to police had increased. In 1923 prosecutors either plea-bargained or dropped more than 28,000 felony counts brought to municipal court.

Dever and his police chief, Morgan Collins, at least made an effort to close speakeasies, raiding Levee bordellos and openly campaigning against bootleggers, but Crowe refused to take an aggressive posture toward enforcing Prohibition laws. A feud between mayor and prosecutor emerged. Capone had many other battles to fight, but he recognized that the hostility between Dever and Crowe only served to divide and weaken the reformers as a political force. As the two politicians clawed at each other, Capone considered the possibility of returning his headquarters to Chicago, where he could solidify his position as gang overlord and political power broker. With the mayor and the state's attorney engaged in a slugfest of headlines and name calling, Al could slip back into the city, reestablish his office near the Levee, and begin to help Big Bill Thompson organize a comeback.

As Al examined this option, the Better Government Association launched yet another broadside on Crowe, accusing him of openly associating with Capone's allies—the

Gennas—and using their muscle to win political favors from Little Italy's voters in the early 1920s.

The attacks on Crowe prompted Illinois Republican senator Charles Deneen to launch an intraparty challenge. With Deneen openly appealing to reformers and winning support from many deep-pocket industrialists and blueblooded bankers, Crowe showed his political skills and tenacity, building a ward-by-ward organization that cranked out voters. Critical parts of his primary-day machinery were supervised by his aides, John Sbarbaro, the prosecutor who doubled as undertaker to gangsters, and William McSwiggin. As Sbarbaro worked the north side—capitalizing on his ties to the remnants of Babyface O'Banion's gang—McSwiggin delivered the west side, relying on his boyhood friends, bootleggers William "Klondike" O'Donnell and his brother, Myles, to turn out voters in the 30th ward.

Unrelated to the south side O'Donnells, Klondike and Myles nevertheless had organized a small, efficient crew that initially allied itself with Capone, but had begun to slice off a bit of its own territory. At first, Capone allowed the minor infractions of territorial agreements, giving the O'Donnells a chance to make a little money of their own. But, they became brave and started to sell beer in Cicero, encouraging saloonkeepers to desert Capone as a supplier. Fully aware that his schoolyard chums were in the bootleg business, McSwiggin continued to socialize with the west side O'Donnells even after he had unsuccessfully prosecuted Myles and gang member Jim Doherty for murder. Though McSwiggin won praise for delivering nine capital convictions, his record of losing gangster cases and his open association with the O'Donnells were precisely the circumstances that caused so many to question the integrity of Crowe's office.

Suspicions grew into open doubts when McSwiggin,

O'Donnell, and Capone frequently crossed paths at various speakeasies and eateries. Boldly violating the law by drinking bootleg beer or liquor, the hanging prosecutor enjoyed a passing acquaintance with Capone, who referred to him as "my friend Billy McSwiggin." On the night of April 17, 1926, McSwiggin went to the Hawthorn Inn and ate dinner with the city's leading gangster. The subject of the sit down remained a mystery, but McSwiggin's father, a police sergeant with thirty years' experience, would later claim to know what was discussed. "If I told," he said, "I'd blow the lid off Chicago."

Nine days later, on the evening of the April 26 primary between the Crowe and Deneen slates, Capone gathered a crew of torpedoes and sluggers and—as some witnesses would later claim—personally handed a tommy gun to one of the men as a car holding McSwiggin, the O'Donnell brothers, and a few others passed into Cicero. All the men were killed in the attack.To this day, it remains a mystery whether Capone gave these orders knowing that McSwiggin was in the Lincoln.

Capone went into hiding, taking cover in Lansing, Michigan, where he split his time between a lakeside retreat and a suite in the Downey Hotel nestled in the shadows of the state capitol.

To sidestep the opposition, Crowe petitioned his political ally and friend Judge William Brothers for the creation of a special grand jury to investigate the McSwiggin murder. Immediately complying, Brothers also granted the panel a huge mandate that would allow Crowe to quietly guide the probe. Under the guise of recusing himself because his role as McSwiggin's boss might make him a potential witness, Crowe won the appointment of another political ally, Illinois Attorney General Oscar Carlstrom, as special prosecutor.

When Carlstrom issued his report in June, he failed to men-

State's Attorney Robert Crowe.

tion Capone, nor did he challenge the O'Donnells. Instead of providing a detailed account of McSwiggin, Carlstrom attacked Crowe's critics. The public, however, refused to accept the state attorney general's findings, and pressure prompted Crowe to petition for another special grand jury, led by former judge Charles McDonald. By mid-July, McDonald and Crowe's chief investigator, Pat Roche, realized that they would have to produce Capone to restore any credibility to the state's attorney. As the organization filtered word to Capone's hideaway in Michigan, Al and his lawyers directly contacted Roche, making plans for his surrender.

On July 28, 1926, a horde of reporters stood with Capone on the Indiana-Illinois state line. While waiting for Roche, Capone held court with the scribes. After he confirmed that he had met with the younger McSwiggin at the Hawthorn Inn and had given the prosecutor a bottle of scotch as a gift for his father the cop, Al boasted, "I paid McSwiggin. I paid him plenty and I got what I paid for."

❖ ❖ ❖

"The real stuff hasn't started."

On July 29, a day after Roche took him into custody, Capone stood before Cook County's chief criminal judge Thomas Lynch, who called on the state to begin proceedings in the murder complaint resulting from Crowe's statement that Capone "handled" the murder weapon.

"Subsequent information," Assistant State's Attorney George Gorman told the court, "could not substantiate this." Lynch dismissed the case, and Capone walked out of the courthouse.

Less than fourteen days after he walked away from charges that he conspired to murder a prosecutor, Capone made his bid for complete control of Chicago's vice and graft.

Through John Torrio's longtime friend, 20th ward boss Morris Eller, Capone learned that Hymie Weiss and Schemer Drucci were to appear at the offices of the Metropolitan Sanitary District on the morning of August 10. Located in one of the city's premier skyscrapers, the Italianate, neo-renaissance Standard Oil Building at 910 South Michigan, the district was a public body that supervised sewerage and water supply—services that provided ample opportunities for ghosting employees, labor racketeering, billing kickbacks, bid rigging, and other forms of corruption. As a successful ward leader, Eller had accumulated enough chits to become a trustee of the district; his position allowed him to share in the agency's graft and wield considerable influence over its operations. As Capone found out, Eller and Assistant State's Attorney John Sbarbaro were to meet Drucci and Weiss to receive a $13,500 payoff to split.

Shortly after breakfast in Drucci's suite at the Congress Hotel, the two hoods walked four blocks south to their appointment. Around 9 A.M., as they approached the tower's bronzed entrance, four men jumped out of a car parked across the street. Brandishing automatic pistols, the quartet opened fire, sending Weiss and Drucci for cover behind another car. Pedestrians shrieked as a full-fledged shootout chipped concrete off buildings and cracked windows. By the time both sides ran out of ammunition, the police appeared on the scene, catching up to Capone gunman Louis Barko in the middle of Michigan Avenue and dragging Drucci off the running board of a passing car. Weiss fled into the Standard Oil Building, and the remaining Capone gunmen sped away. Barko and Drucci were taken to police headquarters, where they refused to identify themselves or each other. When the police asked about the wad of cash in Drucci's pocket, the hood used the opportunity to claim the attack was a botched robbery. "They were after my roll," he told the police. Miraculously, no one was hurt.

Four days later, Weiss and Drucci were driving down Michigan Avenue past the corner that almost became the site of their demise. As their sedan rolled by the Standard Oil Building, a car rammed their rear end and the passengers opened fire. Weiss and Drucci scampered out of their vehicle, shooting over their shoulders.

As headlines trumpeted the battles of the Standard Oil Building, State's Attorney Crowe and Mayor Dever issued empty promises that the gunmen would be hunted down and the rule of law restored. But it was clear to Chicagoans that Al Capone had completely intimidated, bought off, and manipulated the political machinery of an entire city. With newspapers binging on reports of intimidation and violence, citizens were terrified of standing up to hoods who thought nothing of firing hundreds of rounds through a crowd of innocent people going to work. As there were no witnesses willing to come forward, Barko and Drucci were released.

A month later, Weiss and Drucci counterattacked, launching what would be known as the "Bootleg Battle of the Marne." On September 20 at 1 P.M., Weiss, Drucci, and Moran organized a convoy of sedans to enter Cicero and drive by the Hawthorn Inn, where Capone and his bodyguard Frankie Rio sat, sipping coffee after their lunch. Packed with customers who anticipated the track's opening at two-thirty, the eatery broke into a panic when a car passed and the sound of machine-gun fire rattled through the air. Diners ducked under the tables, but Capone realized that the gunmen were firing blanks, because the windows did not shatter. He was determined to confront the hoods who would make such a bold run into his turf and he started for the door, but Rio tackled him.

"It's a stall, boss," he told Capone. "The real stuff hasn't started."

Within a minute, seven cars had pulled up to the Hawthorn Inn, and machine-gun fire began to blast. The Hawthorn Inn and the neighboring Anton Hotel took more than 1,000 rounds, which shattered every pane of glass and tore through every outside doorway. Though no one was killed or wounded inside the buildings, racing enthusiast Clyde Freeman and his wife and son were trapped in their car parked near the hotel during the shooting. Freeman found a bullet hole in his hat and one in his son's coat that did not cause injury, but his wife took a piece of shattered glass in her eye. Upon hearing their cries for help, Capone personally rushed to their car and arranged for hospital treatment, insisting on paying all the bills. Mrs. Freeman required surgery to save her right eye; Capone never questioned the $10,000 bill.

The barrage claimed one other victim, Capone gunman Louis Barko, who was entering the Hawthorn Inn as the first volley began. A bullet seared his shoulder, but he managed to find safety on the ground near the doorway. When hospital officials reported his wound to the police, Barko faced another round of questioning by Shoes Schoemaker, who also grilled Weiss, Drucci, and Moran. Once again, the hoods refused to identify each other—nor would anyone finger a triggerman.

Taking a lesson from Torrio, Capone tried to negotiate a peace with Moran, Drucci, and Weiss. Through Unione Sicilione boss Tony Lombardo, Capone arranged an October 4 meeting at the Morrisson Hotel, and with Lombardo negotiating on his behalf, Capone offered his rivals a chance to distribute beer in half the city—everything north of Madison.

Weiss declined, holding out for a better price. "He's a snake," said Weiss, serving as bargaining agent for the north side crew. "Capone hasn't paid yet for O'Banion's murder."

Lombardo tried to dimiss that killing as being two years old, but Weiss pressed the issue. "Scalise and Anselmi killed O'Banion," Hymie claimed, insisting that the only proof of Capone's sincerity would be a betrayal of the two gunmen.

In his role as negotiator, Lombardo called Capone and relayed Weiss's price for a cease-fire. Rejecting any attempt to turn on his own men, Capone responded, "I wouldn't do that to a yellow dog!" After Lombardo delivered the reply, Weiss walked out.

Four days later, a man who identified himself as Oscar Lundin rented a room overlooking the street and Holy Name Cathedral at a boarding house at 740 State Street, next door to Schofield's Flower Shop, once the home of O'Banion's headquarters. It was the site of his murder and still the preferred meeting place for Weiss, Moran, and Drucci.

On the same day, a young blonde who called herself Mrs. Theodore Schultz rented an apartment at 1 Superior Street that commanded a view of the flower shop and the intersection of State and Superior. From her window, she could see Lundin's room. The next day, Lundin received two male visitors, who took over the room while he vanished. At the same time, two men visited Mrs. Schultz and stayed with her.

Weiss was expected to visit the flower shop on October 11, after spending most of the day at the Criminal Courts building where jury selection had begun in the trial of Polack Joe Saltis and "Lefty" Koncil for the murder of "Mitters" Foley. After court adjourned, Weiss left with four others: his bodyguard and small-time beer runner Paddy Murray, driver Sam Peller, private investigator and 20th ward pol Benny Jacobs, and William O'Brien, a lawyer who served as the lead mouthpiece of the Saltis-Koncil defense team. Around 4 P.M., Peller parked Weiss's Cadillac in front of the Holy Name Cathedral. From the State Street boarding house and the Superior Street apartment, the torpedoes took aim with shotguns and tommy guns.

As Weiss and his men walked to the flower shop, the shooting began. Ten bullets cut down Weiss, while fifteen killed

◈ PROHIBITION ◈

Formally known as the Eighteenth Amendment to the United States Constitution, the ban on the sale of liquor, beer, and wine was ratified on January 16, 1919. Consisting of two parts, this act of Congress was short and simple: Section I read, "After one year from the ratification of this article, the manufacture, sale, or transportation of intoxicating liquors within, the importation thereof into, or the exportation thereof from the United States and all territory subject to the jurisdiction thereof for beverage purposes is hereby prohibited." Section II added, "The Congress and the several States shall have the concurrent power to enforce this article by appropriate legislation."

Prohibition went into effect in 1920 but its passage reflected an effort that had begun in the nineteenth century. Though most of the reform efforts dating to the 1890s were steeped in the struggle to correct the political and economic inequalities of industrial expansion, the ban on alcohol reflected a religious crusade. With the Women's Christian Temperance Union leading the charge against alcohol, a string of midwestern politicians led by Representative Andrew Volstead consolidated their power in Congress, forging a voting bloc around his claim that "law does regulate morality."

As Woodrow Wilson's political coalition was unraveling after World War I, these legislators took advantage of a weak congressional leadership and proposed the ban on alcohol. Politicians were looking toward the 1920 elections. The prohibition amendment—known as the Volstead Act—passed as lawmakers jockeyed for votes throughout the Midwest.

While the WCTU and clerics gloated over the defeat of alcohol, gangsters rejoiced, recognizing that most Americans would eagerly break the law for a beer after work, a glass of wine with dinner, a cocktail before the show. To meet the growing demand for forbidden booze and beer, local gangs were eager to devote considerable energies to mixing their illicit enterprises with legitimate businesses. Throughout major cities, hoods began to cycle their illegal profits into trucking firms, garages, warehouses, restaurants, and meat packing.

Prohibition tripled the revenues of the most successful racketeers within the first few years. Little John

Torrio's organization of brothels and gaming dens netted less than $2 million annually before the ban on alcohol. By the end of 1921, law enforcement officials estimated his organization to gross more than $5 million. Across the country, outlaws learned that bribing the police and delivering whiskey were far more profitable than stickups, bank robberies, or jewel heists. Though a variety of gangs would shoot their way into competition for the lucrative booze trade, Prohibition was the first chance for criminals to cast themselves as men of commerce: They had to manufacture or find the supply of a product, bring it to market, meet a payroll, pay an illicit tax in the form of graft, and then decide how to distribute the profits.

As Al Capone would frequently remind the residents of Chicago, "All I ever did was to sell beer and whiskey to our best people . . . All I ever did was supply a demand that was pretty popular. Why the very guys that make my trade good are the guys who yell the loudest at me."

As Prohibition allowed Capone to fancy himself an entrepreneur, it also undermined authority by forcing millions of Americans to break the law. Instead of prompting citizens to respect police and the role of authority, the ban on alcohol built a double standard into society's system of enforcing and administering justice. Across the land, men and women winked at the law. While hoods and criminal syndicates parlayed booze into their vice rackets, most people who broke Prohibition laws were upstanding citizens who disagreed with public policy. At first the debate over Prohibition took a backseat to other matters. But the continued ban and its open contribution to the well-being of criminals began to eat away at the core of American life.

It would take thirteen years for President Herbert Hoover, Congress, and the state legislatures to repeal Prohibition by passing the Twenty-First Amendment to the United States Constitution. By the time the repeal took effect in 1933, Hoover had lost the White House and Franklin Delano Roosevelt had begun the first of his four terms as president.

Murray. Wounded in his arm, thigh, and stomach, O'Brien dragged himself to the curb. Peller was shot in the groin, Jacobs in the leg. Behind these victims, the cornerstone of the cathedral had been reconfigured. The original bricks had the inscription "A.D. 1874" and a quotation from Philippians 2:10, "At The Name Of Jesus Every Knee Should Bow In Heaven And On Earth"; the shootout changed the wording to ". . . Every Knee . . . In Heaven And On Earth."

Though O'Brien, Peller, and Jacobs eventually recovered, they could not provide any information on their attackers. As the Sbarbaro funeral home prepared for Weiss's funeral, Capone greeted reporters at the newly refurbished and reopened Hawthorn Inn. When asked why the murder of Weiss took place, Capone answered that Babyface O'Banion and Hymie Weiss were killed for the same reason: failing to obey the Torrio-Capone agreements over territory.

A demoralized and frustrated Chief Collins faced the indignity of answering questions about the police's refusal to arrest Capone. "It's a waste of time," Collins said. "He's been in before on other murder charges. He has his alibi."

While Hymie Weiss was laid to rest at a funeral that only drew a few of his gang, Polack Joe Saltis and his partners, Frankie McErlane and "Dingbat" O'Berta, held an urgent meeting: They knew that Capone had discovered their plans to switch beer and liquor suppliers for 200 speakeasies that were under their control. Fearing that their intent to betray would prompt Capone to order their execution, they needed to talk their way out of a jam but were not sure that a direct approach would succeed. O'Berta called labor racketeer Maxie Eisen and mentioned the possibility of a meeting with Capone to iron out differences and pledge loyalty. Eager to help, Eisen suggested a general armistice that would allow the gangsters to meet and once again divide the city into territories.

Within a day, Eisen received an enthusiastic response: Capone would forgive previous grievances and feuds in exchange for a lasting truce that respected neighborhood boundaries.

Capone lieutenants approached a variety of ward heelers, middlemen, bagmen, and hoods in an effort to convene a city-wide gathering of gang leaders for October 21 at the Hotel Sherman, a downtown establishment less than a block away from city hall.

Al called the newsmen, who enjoyed his colorful quotes, to leak word of the meeting, a move designed to further highlight his importance at the session. With reporters outside the room and photographers taking pictures of those who came in and out, more than thirty hoods attended the meeting. Mingling among the reporters were police officers in uniform and detectives, who occasionally walked up to a hood and spoke as if they were businessmen going to an appointment.

Within an hour, Capone presented his plan for a five-point armistice that would cement his position as leader of the largest gang and overseer of relations throughout the city: First, he called for a general amnesty to bury all outstanding feuds and vendettas; second, a rejection of violence to settle disputes and the establishment of arbitration to resolve them; third, an end to using the press and police gossip as a means of "ribbing" or bluffing that one gangster was planning to move against another; fourth, complete respect for territorial boundaries regarding customers of bootleg beer and booze; fifth, for the head of each gang to punish his members who violate the terms of the pact.

After forging a consensus on these general principles, Capone set forth his division of the city's turfs. The O'Banionites were to retreat from all territory acquired outside their original power base in the 42nd and 43rd wards. By leaving the north side gang this thickly populated area near the lake-front and Lincoln Park, Capone gave Moran and Drucci a small but extremely lucrative franchise that catered to gold coast residents and other high rollers. Saltis, McErlane, and O'Berta were to split southwest Chicago with the gang operated by Ralph Sheldon—a move that penalized Polack Joe for being disloyal and taking steps to side with Weiss. As for his own organization, Capone gave himself all of the center, southern, and western portions of the city's core—a territory that included 20,000 speakeasies and eateries. He also held on to the suburbs.

Despite the uneven split, Capone's rivals were in no position to raise a serious dissent: Capone had the money and muscle to get anything he wanted. As the participants signed on to what would become known as the "Hotel Sherman Treaty," Capone met the press. "I told them we're making a shooting gallery out of a great business," he said. "Why not put up our guns and treat our business like any other man treats his, as something to work at in the daytime and forget when he goes home at night? There's plenty of beer business for every-body—why kill each other over it?"

With Chicagoans recognizing Capone's power, he turned his eye toward returning the gangsters' pal, Republican Big Bill Thompson, to city hall. Democratic fortunes were waning under the inabilities of Mayor William Dever to conquer crime, and his bid for reelection was weak, so Republicans jumped at the chance. As a result of the battles of the Standard Oil Building and the shootout that claimed Moran's life, three GOP candidates scrambled through a primary: Edward Litsinger, a reformer supported by Senator Charles Deneen, ran on a strict Prohibition and good government platform; Dr. John Dill Robertson, a former health commissioner, stood with a faction supported by convicted felon and former congressman Fred Lundin; and Thompson, who campaigned on a platform that openly proclaimed his support for liquor, speakeasies, women, and music.

"I'm wetter than the middle of the Atlantic Ocean," Big Bill bellowed to the applause of his supporters. In a campaign full of stunts that included christening a yacht and renting a theater for a performance that featured Thompson holding up dead rats when calling out the names of his political adversaries, the former mayor used his clowning to capture the voters' imagination. While his rivals addressed the mounting threat to public safety or the city's overextended infrastructure, Big Bill kept to jingoistic sloganeering. When Thompson's rivals pointed to his close associations with gangsters and outlaws, his corrupt administrations, his flip-flops—distancing himself from State's Attorney Robert Crowe and once again embracing him during primary season—Big Bill launched a barrage of personal attacks that succeeded in diverting voter attention. He told them that Robertson was a slob who spilled soup through his whiskers and onto his vest; to make matters worse, Big Bill claimed, Robertson never bathed, and his odor earned him the moniker Dr. John Dill Pickle. As for Litsinger, Big Bill attacked his virility and manhood by insisting that this candidate played handball wearing tight pants or "little shorts." Using his hands to demonstrate the small size of these garments, Thompson called Litsinger an inexperienced waif or boy in a man's world of rough-and-tumble politics.

Less than two weeks after the gangsters resolved their differences at the Hotel Sherman, Republicans gave Thompson a

180,000-vote primary victory that qualified him to run for mayor in the municipal elections of April 1927.

❖ ❖ ❖

". . .Gomorrah on a Saturday afternoon."

With Thompson leading the Republican ticket, Capone anted up more than $250,000 toward the final campaign and relocated his headquarters to the Hotel Metropole, a seven-story fortress of brick and granite at the corner of 23rd Street and Michigan Avenue. Less than two blocks away from the Four Deuces and his old haunts in the Levee, the Metropole had initially served as an occasional hideaway when Capone wanted to spend a night in the city. Now, Thompson's campaign and the gangland truce provided Al with the opportunity to work openly in Chicago.

To provide for his needs, Capone rented a fourth-floor suite of eight rooms. Behind a huge mahogany desk, he installed a thronelike swivel chair, which some gangsters believed to be fitted with an armor plate in the back. To his close associates, Capone confided that the elaborate chair, with its bronze legs and eagle wing ornaments, reminded him of his boyhood shoe-shine squabbles. Al insisted that his office have an indestructible seat. "To Al, this chair was very symbolic," said his piano-playing pal, Jack Woodford. "He said to me many, many times: 'Professor, if that punk had not broken my chair, I'd still be shining shoes.'"

Throughout the late winter and early spring of 1927, Capone eschewed any outburst of violence that would give

Dever and his reformers a campaign issue that might derail Thompson's bid for power. The only exception came on March 11, when Capone sanctioned punishment against Polack Joe Saltis for gunning down a rival beer runner. Capone's gunners killed Lefty Koncil and Charlie "Big Hayes" Hubacek. By murdering two gunmen as retaliation for the killing of one beer runner, Capone told the underworld that he would inflict a 2-for-1 price upon any violations of the truce.

Though most of Chicago's gangsters understood the message, Schemer Drucci still wanted to topple Capone. In late March, he followed Al's entourage to their vacation spot in Hot Springs, Arkansas. As Capone made his way around the resort, an errant shotgun blast rang out, missing him. Once again, Capone waited to seek his revenge.

Without involving him, it came on the day before the municipal elections, April 4, 1927. Capone had ordered his goons off the streets to help the electorate "to vote early and vote often." Al's underworld opponents took the opposite tactic. Though they also wanted a Thompson victory, Moran and Drucci figured they could help by more overt and violent means. On the afternoon before the balloting was to begin, Drucci demanded an audience with 42nd ward alderman Dorsey Crowe (no relation to State's Attorney Robert Crowe), a Dever supporter. When the secretary announced that Crowe was out of the office, Drucci went on a rampage, beating up the woman, overturning her desk, and destroying files.

The cops overtook Drucci and two of his cohorts on the corner of Diversey and Clark. Subdued by Detective Daniel Healy, an officer who relished showdowns with gangsters, Drucci was disarmed, cuffed, and taken to the precinct lockup. Word of the arrest reached Drucci's mouthpiece, Maurice

Green, who demanded that his client be arraigned before a judge and given the opportunity to post bail. Tossed into a squad car with Healy and three other cops, Drucci found himself the subject of repeated taunts. The detective was eager to needle the hood, so he removed Drucci's cuffs and pointed a revolver at his chest. Drucci began to talk back.

"I'll get you," Drucci reportedly told the detective. "I'll wait on your doorstep."

"Shut your mouth," Healy replied.

"Go on kid copper," Drucci dared, in reference to the gun. "I'll fix you."

"Keep quiet," said the cop.

"You take your gun off me or I'll kick the hell out of you."

At that moment, Healy claimed, Drucci "got up on one leg and struck me on the side of the head, saying, 'I'll take you and your tool.'"

When Drucci grabbed Healy's right hand, the detective switched the gun to his left hand and fired four shots. Drucci died before the cops reached the Criminal Courts building.

Green demanded that Healy be arrested for murder, but Chief of Detectives Shoes Schoemaker would never allow the prosecution of a cop for killing a renowned gangster. Since the 1925 shooting of Frank Capone, Chicago cops had not taken down a gangster of significance despite the attacks on several policemen.

But afraid that Drucci's killing would incite violence on election day, Police Chief Collins deployed more than 5,000 cops to stand guard at every polling place. Special squads of detectives patrolled the streets in flivvers equipped with machine guns and tear gas cannisters. The overwhelming show of force kept the elections relatively quiet—two bombings directed at the 42nd ward Democrats, two kidnappings of election officials, a drive-by shooting attack on one polling place, and a handful of Dever supporters confronted by thugs with guns.

After Thompson tallied the returns of his 83,000-vote victory from the ballroom of the Hotel Sherman, he invited hundreds of his supporters to join him in a party on his yacht, *Big Bill*, moored in Belmont Harbor. As the revelers flooded the ship's cypress deck, the boat teetered from one side to the next and eventually capsized. The party continued as the soaked celebrants retrieved cases of bootleg whiskey and barrels of beer from the sunken boat.

In the following days newspapers trumpeted Healy as a hero, but gangsters heard another version of Drucci's killing. Word began to spread that Healy was part of the extensive net-

The Hotel Metropole, Capone's headquarters.

BIG BILL THOMPSON

WILLIAM HALE "BIG BILL" THOMPSON, CHICAGO'S MOST OUTRAGEOUS MAYOR.

He was a Boston brahmin who became the pawn of Chicago's gangsters. Born in 1867, William Hale "Big Bill" Thompson hailed from a long line of military and naval officers who left the east to stake their fortune in real estate. The elder Thompson wanted his son to follow the family footsteps at elite boarding schools and eastern colleges, but Big Bill preferred the wide open spaces of Utah, Wyoming, and Nebraska. Instead of completing his education in Cambridge, Princeton, or New Haven, the young man wandered the plains and prairies. When his father summoned him to Chicago in the 1880s, Big Bill enrolled in a local business college and began to work for the family.

By the early 1890s, Big Bill had inherited a fortune in cash and downtown real estate. A strapping six feet, five inches tall and sporting a handlebar mustache, he was known throughout the city for his feats in amateur track and football competitions. After a colleague bet him $50, Thompson submitted his name for second ward alderman on the 1900 slate posted by the nonpartisan Municipal Voters League. To everyone's surprise, his gregarious character, his good-time Charlie persona, and his loud, booming voice allowed Thompson to cast himself as a formidable orator and stump politician. He entertained the voters and frequently fed off their ethnic prejudices: His trademark involved standing before groups of Irish voters and attacking the House of Windsor. Within two years, he became a Republican candidate for Cook County commissioner.

Thompson's steady rise through the party ranks was accompanied by repeated brushes with scandal. The

Amateur Athletic Union expelled him for a payola scam that bordered on game fixing; testimony in a civil suit revealed that he regularly patronized Levee bordellos; and he portrayed himself as a devoted family man even though his Jewish mistress accompanied him on official business.

By 1915, Big Bill had won the mayoralty by the largest margin ever recorded for a Republican. Within months, gangsters recognized that city hall was open for business: The newly elected mayor launched his Sportsmen's Club, which solicited $100 "life memberships" from every tavern owner, madam, bookie, businessman, alderman, city official, hoodlum, and grifter in the city. In exchange for the donation, the individual received a card that proved handy when seeking city services or facing the police. The club's directors, featured on its letterhead, included Police Chief Charles Healy, slot machine manufacturer Herbert Mills, gaming den owner Mort Tennes, and Big Jim Colosimo. In a show of the club's clout, Thompson ordered Healy to disband the city's vice squad after detectives raided a cathouse owned by one of the members.

After eight years of unprecedented corruption, voters in 1923 turned to Mayor William "Decent" Dever, a Democrat who spent most of his four-year term crusading against gangsters. But Capone and his rivals frustrated Dever at every turn, and the citizenry grew tired and disillusioned with "reform"; the Republicans turned to Thompson one more time in 1927. With the open support of Al Capone, Thompson cruised back into office and bootleggers ushered in their last run at prosperity.

"Big Bill Thompson was completely corrupt," said reform alderman Charles Merriam, who was also a political science professor at the University of Chicago. "And he made sure that his government would keep Chicago completely corrupt from the cop on the beat, to the city councilor on the take, to judges and most of all himself."

When Capone fell, so did Thompson, replaced by Anton Cermak, who started what would become the legendary Democratic machine of Chicago. As corruption would become a staple of Chicago's politics, Thompson retreated from the public eye. When he died in March 1944, he left an estate valued at more than $2 million, an astonishing sum for a former mayor who never earned more than $22,500 per year.

work of cops owned by the Capone organization. Though Al would not discuss Drucci's death, many hoods wondered if Capone had paid Healy a premium for taking out Schemer. According to Woodford, who had pieces of inside information, Drucci's squad-car assault on Healy was a fiction manufactured to cover up a cold-blooded assassination. Woodford insisted Detective Daniel Healy was on Capone's payroll.

"Capone didn't order the killing, Ralph Capone did. . . . Al indulged in homicide only as a last resort."

A week after Thompson's swearing in, Capone enlarged his Hotel Metropole headquarters to fifty rooms.

First, acting as if he were mayor himself, Capone decided to end the reign of Bathhouse John Coughlin and Hinky Dink Kenna as first ward committeemen and power brokers. Summoning them to his suite, he bluntly demanded their resignation. Coughlin and Kenna quietly accepted the terms of their surrender, thankful that they weren't executed. "My God, what could I say?" Kenna told a small group of his followers. "We're lucky to get as good a break as we did."

Second, Capone solidified his relationship with the police and the press by beginning to pay a weekly stipend to *Chicago Tribune* reporter Jake Lingle. As the *Trib*'s police reporter, Lingle had access to Police Chief Hughes, Chief of Detectives Shoes Schoemaker, and dozens of captains, lieutenants, and sergeants; as such, Capone knew that Lingle could serve as a valuable intermediary for messages, gossip, and tips concerning betrayals, double crosses, and sellouts.

Third, Capone established regular office hours on Sunday mornings and afternoons at the Metropole, where he wanted to meet and hear the concerns of his employees or parties interested in obtaining his assistance. Like a potentate holding court, Capone encouraged lawyers, politicians, union bosses, judges, cops, and others to seek him out and request favors.

In a rare display of his clout that mixed public ceremony, official business, and ethnic pride, Capone proudly joined Mayor Thompson's official delegation to welcome Francesco de Pinedo, the Italian transatlantic pilot who landed his hydroplane on Lake Michigan. As a personal emissary of Italian dictator Benito Mussolini, de Pineda brought official greetings from the Italian government and people. Capone was one of the first to shake the pilot's hand and welcome him ashore. After reformers questioned the propriety of a gangster serving in the city's official delegation, Police Chief Hughes told the press that Capone was invited because his standing in the city's Italian community could help quell an antifascist riot if one ever broke out.

As the newspapers focused on this lame excuse, reporters overlooked a new office created in the bowels of city hall. Labeled the Commission on Wharves and put under the direction of Harry Bergman—an acquaintance of Greasy Thumb Guzik—the three-room suite housed several of Capone's torpedoes and spies who kept watch on Big Bill and his pals. "After this," Woodford recalled, "the town was more wide open than Gomorrah on a Saturday afternoon."

circa 1928

CHAPTER FIVE

TOP OF THE WORLD

O ne month after Big Bill's victory lifted Capone to the height of his powers, Associate Justice Oliver Wendell Holmes of the Supreme Court inadvertently began the process that would lead to the gangster's demise. In a case brought from Charleston, South Carolina, the justices were asked to rule on the government's claim that illegal income had to be reported to the Internal Revenue Service and be subject to taxes. According to the court files, the taxmen went after Charleston bootlegger Manely Sullivan, who refused to declare his illicit income. His lawyers argued that the Fifth Amendment privilege protecting self-incrimination exempted a crook from declaring his income and thereby revealing the nature of his illegal activities. Holmes and a majority of the court disagreed.

The ruling made headlines across the nation, but Capone shrugged it off. Banking on the gangster's cocky disdain, however, was an overly diligent, humble yet tenacious civil servant, Elmer Irey, a former postal stenographer who had clawed his way to become chief of the IRS's Special Intelligence Unit. Working with the Secret Service and other Treasury Department agents, this elite group of agents immediately understood the ramifications of Holmes's opinion: They could fight the hoods with new weapons—ledgers and accountants, bookkeepers and bank statements, instead of tommy guns and pistols.

In Chicago, Irey assembled a team of field agents that centered around Nels Tessem, an actuarial wizard who enjoyed the challenge of sifting through financial statements; Arthur Madden, who often played the role of tough cop in seizing or demanding the production of bank records, checks, and receipts; and Archie Madden, who specialized in learning the ins and outs of Chicago's bootlegging turfs. To supervise the group, Irey assigned Frank Wilson, a stone-faced former real estate agent from Buffalo who chomped on nickel cigars and reportedly "sweat ice water." Despite the bureaucratic tugs-of-war between the Treasury Department and the Department of Justice, Irey's efforts received an unexpected boost when President Coolidge named a taciturn lawyer of Swedish-American stock, George E. Q. Johnson Jr., the U.S. attorney for the district of Northern Illinois. Aware of the citywide corruption and sickened by bootleggers' mockery of the law, Johnson was committed to using federal resources to restore integrity to local government.

From the beginning Irey wanted to go after Capone, but he understood that his agents had to start at the bottom and work their way up through the gang. Wilson's IRS crew figured that their first targets should be Terry Druggan and Frank Lake, the legitimate fronts who initially agreed to partner with Johnny Torrio in the brewing of beer.

As Capone openly embarked on a campaign of high-profile public appearances at ballparks, boxing matches, concert halls and nightclubs, a dissident faction of the Unione Sicilione plotted his demise. Led by Joseph Aiello and his brothers, who had used their muscle to take over the Little Italy stills and the moonshine business, this rebellious group mounted several attempts to kill Capone and his Sicilian ally Tony Lombardo. Arising out of Capone's decision to install Lombardo as head of the Unione, this feud was rooted in Aiello's belief that the Neapolitan Capone would never give the Sicilians their due. But Capone's vast network of crooked cops and thieves, hustlers and bootleggers picked up on Aiello's discontent and repeatedly tipped off Capone to his rival's moves, with bloody consequences for Aiello's men.

Within the first months of Big Bill's term, his police chief Michael Hughes and the newly appointed chief of detectives, William O'Connor, faced eleven gangland killings that were connected and unsolved. To answer the public outcry for special tactics, Hughes and O'Connor announced the formation of special armored squad cars and patrols consisting of cops who had fought overseas. Besides offering these men the latest in police vehicles, Hughes and O'Connor equipped them with machine guns. "It is the wish of the people of Chicago that you hunt these criminals down," O'Connor told the first squad in a well-publicized ceremony.

While the rhetoric made great copy for the newspapers and provided Mayor Thompson and Police Chief Hughes with the appearance of fighting gangsters, O'Connor came to believe in his own publicity stunts. In a strange twist of events, the chief of detectives found himself in the position of actually delivering competent police services to the city. Without firing a single round, his special squads uncovered an interconnected series of hideouts and gunning nests that had been set up to further inflame the feud between Capone and Aiello. On November 22, 1927, O'Connor's men were alerted to a possible assassination of Tony Lombardo, scheduled to take place as the Unione Sicilione boss walked up the steps to his home at 442 West Washington Boulevard north of Cicero. Taking a

Louis "Little New York" Campagna (center). Like Capone, a New York gangster transplanted to Chicago.

number of machine guns out of the apartment across the street, the detectives made their next move at 7002 North Western Avenue, where they uncovered a stash of dynamite and a key to a room at the Rex Hotel on Ashland Avenue. As they staked out the room, the cops came upon Milwaukee-based triggerman Angelo Lo Mantino and Joey Aiello, who were taken to police headquarters.

When Capone's crooked cops heard of the pinch, they told their boss, who sent more than a dozen men to ring the building. Capone's hoods then sent Louis "Little New York" Campagna into the main entrance. Campagna was known as one of the gang's toughest, a throwback who worked his way through Manhattan's Five Pointers and then came to the Midwest, where he immediately struck a chord with the transplanted New Yorker, Capone. As Campagna entered the detective bureau escorted by two other hoods, he deliberately opened his overcoat and displayed his shouldered revolver. He did not resist when they arrested him.

Naively believing that they had diffused a violent confrontation, the police brass obliged Campagna by putting him in the cell next to Aiello. Within minutes, Little New York broke into a Sicilian dialect directed to Capone's rival. "You're dead, friend, you're dead," Campagna kept repeating. "You won't get up to the end of the street still walking."

"Can't we settle this?" Aiello answered. "Give me fourteen days and I'll sell my stores, my house and everything and quit Chicago for good. Think of my wife and baby!"

"You dirty rat," shot back Campagna, coining a phrase that actor Jimmy Cagney would later make famous. "You've broken faith with us twice now. You started this. We'll finish it."

When Aiello's lawyer arranged his release, reporters overheard the Sicilian thug seeking protection from O'Connor, the

Irish cop. Though Aiello pleaded for help to get out of town, O'Connor only offered a couple of detectives to walk the hood into a taxi. Upon leaving the police station, Aiello and his brothers, Dominic and Tony, made it to Trenton, where they kept a low profile for two years before their return.

Newsmen did not know Aiello's destination but they quickly understood that his disappearance was one more victory for Capone. He did not mince words. "I'm the boss," he insisted. "I'm going to run things. They've been putting the roscoe on me for a good many years and I'm still healthy and happy. Don't let anyone kid you into thinking I can be run out of town. When we get through with this mob, there won't be any opposition and I'll still be doing business."

❧ ❧ ❧

"I'm sick of the job."

From his throne on the fourth floor of the Metropole, the twenty-eight-year-old Capone mistakenly believed he had enough clout to overcome anything, but a surprising political twist turned the end of 1927 into a series of missteps and miscalculations. When President Calvin Coolidge declared that he would not seek reelection, Mayor Big Bill Thompson immediately cast himself as a candidate. To show the country that his police department could and would crack down on bootleggers and hoods, Big Bill ordered Police Chief Hughes and Chief of Detectives O'Connor to begin a harassment campaign that would round up thugs on any possible charge.

While most Chicagoans saw the presidential escapade as one more bit of Big Bill's buffoonery, press baron William Randolph Hearst jumped on the bandwagon, lending an aura of credibility to Thompson's nascent but eventually short-lived bid for the GOP presidential nomination.

Hearst's support immediately drew the attention of State's Attorney Robert Crowe, who had endured ups and downs with Thompson and Chicago's rackets. Recognizing that the country's largest newspaper publisher had bestowed the mayor with a national platform, Crowe made sure that he fell in line. Chicagoans knew that Crowe had openly broken with Big Bill over the prosecution of Fred Lundin, but now the prosecutor wanted to make peace and appear as a loyal lieutenant in the city's army of Republicans. Upon Thompson's return from a private audience at Hearst's California ranch, Crowe gave an interview to the press baron's *Chicago Herald-Examiner* and its sister, the *Chicago American* in which he praised Thompson.

The double talk angered Capone, and he refused Thompson's request to remain quiet. Though Al knew that Hughes's crackdown was intended as show business for voters and reporters, he decided to speak. "I've been spending the best years of my life as a public benefactor," Capone told the *Chicago Tribune.* "I've given people the light pleasures, shown them a good time. And all I get is abuse—the existence of a hunted man. I'm called a killer." Unwilling to pass up the chance to portray himself as a straight-shooting rogue, Capone continued, "There's one thing worse than a crook and that's a crooked man in a big political job."

While most of Chicago's politicians gagged on such a brazen assessment of their value, they remained quiet when Capone announced that he would leave town. Of course, he had no intention of relinquishing control of the organization that netted more than $100 million in 1927, yet Capone went through the motions of calling it quits. "Let the worthy citizens of Chicago get their liquor the best way they can," he said. "I'm sick of the job."

The publicity stunt backfired. When Al announced that he was leaving town for St. Petersburg, Florida, an emboldened Chief Hughes ordered the cops to arrest him if he were ever to return. Feasting on Hughes's bold stance, the newspapers and wire services encouraged lawmen all over the country to issue similar ultimatums. At various points on the train route between Illinois and Florida, police chiefs and sheriffs vowed to harass the Capone party. Eager to get their boasts in print, the cops tipped their hand, so Capone instead boarded a train for Los Angeles, hoping to send for his wife and son at a later date. On December 13, 1927, he checked into the Hotel Biltmore under the alias Al Brown, but the Los Angeles police chief James Davis surprised him and ordered him out of town. "I thought you people liked tourists," Al told a horde of reporters as he waited to board the eastbound *Santa Fe Chief* on December 14. "Whoever heard of anybody being run out of Los Angeles that had money."

Chicago's newspapers boldly displayed Capone's departure, and Police Chief Hughes once again raised the stakes, promising to arrest the hood as soon as he returned to the city. When Capone alit from the train in Joliet, he expected to meet his brother Ralph. Instead, Capone stepped into the sights of Joliet police chief John Corcoran. "Pleased to meet you," Capone wisecracked, surrendering his .45-caliber automatic, a smaller pistol, and the ammunition as he looked into the barrels of the shotguns. "What's the artillery for?"

Booked on the charge of carrying a concealed weapon, Capone spent less than twelve hours in the lockup. But his armor had been dented.

To avoid another encounter with the law, Capone was ferried

❖ THE PRESS ❖

He loved reporters and they returned his affection with a river of ink and a mountain of newsprint. For Al Capone, the competition among Chicago's major dailies was often better than the action at the racetrack at Hialeah. Once he had inherited John Torrio's organization and saw that front-page headlines offered a means of boosting his influence, Capone became the first gangster to understand the power of the mass media.

"He knew how our business worked," recalled Ben Hecht. "He understood how one scribe had to beat another, like a street corner boast. It was a natural for him to call over each one of us and give us something a little different.

"He knew the truth didn't matter, only the competition."

According to Hecht—who would use Capone as a model for his character in the script of the pioneering gangster movie *Scarface*, Al made a point of knowing reporters by name and ingratiating himself with the press. Like a politician who had to directly communicate with voters, Capone saw reporters as the vehicle for pleading his case against the rigidity of Prohibition and reformers.

"He knew that we were just a bunch of card-playing, cigar-smoking guys who wanted to drink and go out with pretty women," added Hecht. "He knew how to appeal to us as individuals and that's why so many reporters tripped over each other to get a Capone story a day."

"Sure, the stories were sensational and full of all the classic tabloid tricks," noted *Chicago Sun Times* executive John Trezvant in 1967. "But the press made Al Capone into a real character, a human being that people could have an image of. He wanted people to see him in a certain way and sometimes he conned reporters into doing his bidding.

"On many occasions, we had the chance to show him as who he was—a murderous rogue who used his rage to terrorize the whole city. In some ways that's why he will always have a hold on the imagination of those who live here; he was the first gangster who gave newspapers the chance to really portray the people, the individuals, who chose to lead the life of organized crime."

home through Chicago Heights, a suburb controlled by his ally Frankie LaPorte. Though the Chicago chief of detectives O'Connor repeated his promise to arrest Capone, his officers backed off from a direct confrontation. Instead, they shadowed him and openly patrolled the house at 7244 Prairie. As he shuffled back and forth from the Metropole, he drew a police escort—another sign of humiliation. On December 22, Capone pleaded guilty to the charge of carrying a concealed weapon. In exchange for his plea, he was fined $2,601, which he paid with twenty-seven C-notes. When the clerk tried to give him change, Capone insisted that the remainder be given to charity.

As the year 1928 began, Capone tried to reverse his luck; he boarded a train bound for Miami, where he checked himself into the elegant Hotel Ponce de Leon and rented a beachside home for Mae and Sonny. When the press discovered his whereabouts, Capone cast himself as yet "another sucker" looking to leave the north. "I am going to build or buy a home here," he told the newsmen, praising Miami as "the garden of America, the sunny Italy of the New World, where life is good and abundant, where happiness can be enjoyed by even the poorest."

To allay fears that Capone would turn Miami into another Cicero, Mayor J. Newton Lummus summoned him to his office. During their cordial session, Capone made it clear that he had no intention of opening any gaming parlor or vice spot in Miami. Expressing his desire to have a safe vacation home and send his son to school, Capone dangled a hefty commission in front of Lummus, who was also a licensed real estate agent, if he would help find the right property. The mayor was ready to earn his cut. First, he arranged for the Miami police chief H. Leslie Quigg to tell reporters that Al could stay in the city if he obeyed the law and abstained from participating in any of

Al Capone's car, circa 1928.

the local rackets. Then, he began the process of selling Capone the fourteen-room, Spanish-style Palm Island mansion built by Clarence Busch in 1922. Aware that his efforts on behalf of Capone required discretion, Mayor Lummus also participated in a series of shadow transactions that allowed Capone to launder the cash needed to pay for the house.

Reporters and the public quickly discovered that Capone had purchased a residence on Biscayne Bay. Photographs of the private beach, the stucco facade, and Al's new boat, named after his son and nephew, were published across the country. Mae Capone avoided the press limelight, but she was known throughout Miami's shopping district, decorating the first home she did not have to share with her parents, her in-laws, or other family members. From copies of Louis XIV antiques to gold, rimmed porcelain plates, she outfitted the home in the manner of overstuffed royalty. After spending $40,000 to purchase the property, Capone spent another $100,000 on furnishings and renovations. In paying for these items, Al and Mae drew cash out of a wooden chest nestled beside their king-size bed. His underworld business would force Al to shuttle back and forth from this home, but he encouraged Mae and Sonny to settle in.

While Miami welcomed the high-rolling Capones, the hard guys in Chicago took advantage of the boss's absence. At first, trouble appeared to be a minor skirmish in the Republican party, when the reformers led by Senator Charles Deneen announced that they would run John Swanson as a challenge to State's Attorney Robert Crowe. Deneen may have enjoyed the luxury of presenting himself as a thoroughbred reformer who disdained rough-and-tumble politics, but the senator in fact had a long and fruitful relationship with Diamond Joe Esposito, the owner of the Bella Napoli Cafe and an effective Republican ward boss. Having fought Crowe and his faction in a number of intraparty squabbles, Esposito once again relished the prospect of unseating the state's attorney.

❖ ❖ ❖

"The police are with us."

On January 27, a bomb exploded at the home of Charles Fitzmorris, the Thompson crony who served as police chief in the mayor's first two terms and city controller in his third. Thirty minutes after this explosion, another bomb rocked the home of Thompson's commissioner of public service, Dr. William Reid. Deneen and Swanson were among the first to denounce the attacks, but it was obvious to Thompson and Crowe that the explosions marked the beginning of a long and violent primary season.

As the political situation spun out of control, Capone made

the mistake of delaying his return, unwilling to inflame the situation with his presence. His absence, however, prompted rival gangsters to escalate the violence. Reporters wrote that each faction had procured specialists in assembling "pineapples," the prickly, hand-held explosives that were tossed like grenades. With bombings becoming a regular feature of the campaign, headline writers dubbed the election "the pineapple primary."

At each turn, Crowe and Thompson used the explosions to insist that Esposito and other Swanson loyalists were behind the tactics of violence and intimidation. But these claims rang hollow to an electorate that was familiar with Big Bill's insistence on standing up for bootleggers and his pride in having Capone officially represent the city. As for Crowe, voters believed his years as state's attorney were repeatedly compromised by the ambiguous dealings of Assistant State's Attorney McSwiggin, the failure to convict gangsters on murder charges, and the open refusal to enforce Prohibition laws.

Capone began to see that public sentiment was rising against Big Bill and Crowe. There was no percentage in returning to Chicago and backing a loser. At the same time, a Swanson victory would force Capone and his organization to forge a new relationship with a state's attorney dedicated to prosecuting anyone who was allied with Thompson.

The situation grew worse on March 21 when a Capone lieutenant, acting on his own, telephoned a threat to Esposito at his café. Though his wife, Carmela, and bodyguards Ralph and Joe Varchetti implored Diamond Joe to avoid a meeting at his Republican clubhouse, Esposito refused to be intimidated. After the gathering broke up, Esposito walked home with his men. As his wife watched from the window, a car rolled in from behind and three men opened fire with two shotguns and a pistol. The Varchettis ducked but Diamond Joe fell in a pool of his own blood. He died in Carmela's arms.

Even though the cops and rival thugs believed that Capone did not order the hit, they were overjoyed when the newspapers' speculations blamed Al. Capone now realized that his silence and low profile had given him no choice but to lamely protest his innocence in the court of public opinion. To Swanson and Deneen, the killing of Esposito gave them the opportunity to link Capone to Crowe's campaign. The newspapers thirsted for any angle that implicated Al in the pineapple primary.

A day after Senator Deneen led Esposito's funeral procession, a bomb exploded at his three-story house. That night, Swanson dodged a bomb tossed at his car. "The criminal element is trying to dominate Chicago by setting up a dictatorship in politics," Deneen said of Capone, allowing the reporters to

Capone's Palm Island estate, which once belonged to beer magnate Charles Busch.

infer that Al was orchestrating the campaign of terror from his luxurious palace in Miami.

Like Capone, Thompson and Crowe could not dig themselves out of this public relations nightmare. The bombings at the homes of a senator and judge became national and international news. When the polls opened on April 10, Capone made the fatal error of directing his goons to work for Crowe. Besides creating fraudulent votes, they destroyed ballots marked for Swanson and intimidated voters who expressed their preference for reform. When a few voters complained to the cops assigned to stand guard, Capone ally Morris Eller, boss of the 20th ward, told the dissidents, "The police are with us."

On the morning of April 11 the voters of Chicago woke up to find that the Republicans had given Crowe his last verdict. Of the more than 800,000 ballots counted, the overwhelming majority were for Swanson.

Thompson drowned his sorrows and took an official leave of absence, turning over his duties to corporation counsel Samuel Ettleson, who became acting mayor. Jarred by the defeat, Capone retreated to Miami.

After the defeat of Crowe, Capone quietly focused on business. He learned that a number of trucks that had started out in Brooklyn had been hijacked before they had even left the borough. Frankie Yale was suspected. If these accusations were true, Yale was selling booze to Capone with one hand, then stealing from him with the other and reselling the stock. The possibility of an old friend initiating a double cross enraged Capone, and he dispatched a spy, James "Jimmy Files" Finsey de Amato, to Brooklyn. De Amato quickly discovered evidence that Yale had sanctioned the hijackings. Days later, de Amato was gunned down in the street.

Throughout June, Capone laid his plans to kill the man who

had helped launch his underworld career. Having returned to Miami on June 17, he made sure his whereabouts were easily documented. At the same time, he asked his Miami-based friend, Parker Henderson Jr., to order six revolvers and six shotguns from a Fort Worth gun dealer. By the third week of the month, Capone was playing host to Jack Guzik, Dan Seritella, Fred Burke, Jack McGurn, Albert Anselmi, and John Scalise.

After Henderson received the guns, he stashed them in an empty room at the Hotel Ponce de Leon, where the gangsters picked them up. On June 28 Burke, McGurn, Anselmi, and Scalise boarded the *Southland Express*, ostensibly heading for Chicago. They got off at Knoxville, Tennessee, and bought a used Nash sedan for $1,050 in cash. Then, the quartet headed for New York. Capone remained in Miami.

As the triggermen closed in on Brooklyn, the *Miami Daily News* published a story that detailed how Mayor Lummus and Henderson fronted for Capone. The article angered the City Council, which passed a resolution labeling Capone "an undesirable resident by reason of his reputed connection" with the Chicago rackets. In calling for Lummus to resign, the councilors also insisted that Capone's presence in Miami was to the "moral detriment" of the community. Within a day, newspapers across the country were carrying the story of how Miami was seeking to bounce Capone. Reporters flocked to his home; he gladly entertained them, believing that the newsmen would provide him with a great alibi when Yale was killed.

On Sunday, July 1, a telephone call summoned Yale out of a Brooklyn speakeasy in the early afternoon. Wearing a light gray suit and a Panama hat, he jumped into his new Lincoln. But as he drove off, he failed to notice the car that began to follow him. When the sedan began to pull alongside, Yale realized that he was a target. Taking a sharp turn onto 44th Street, Yale screeched into the midst of Solomon and Bertha Kauffman's party in honor of their son's bar mitzvah. The guests saw the second car, a shotgun protruding from the window. After a blast, the Lincoln rolled out of control. To finish the job, a machine gun in the second car fired away. When the Lincoln came to a halt, the door swung open and a bloody Frankie Yale tumbled onto the street. It was the first time that a tommy gun was used in a New York murder.

At the corner of 36th Street between Second and Third avenues in Brooklyn, the gunmen abandoned their car along with two .45-caliber revolvers and the machine gun—which were recovered by the cops. As 100,000 people turned out for Yale's funeral, detectives worked overtime, tracing the serial numbers on the revolvers to the Fort Worth dealer, the tommy gun to Peter von Frantzius's sporting goods store in Chicago. Following the paper trail through Texas, the New York cops came to the southern tip of Florida, where Parker Henderson Jr. had already wilted in the heat from the newspaper's exposé of his laundering money for Capone. Within a week of the murder, Henderson told authorities that he had purchased the weapons at Capone's request. On July 8, 1928, the *Chicago Tribune* carried the headline "Yale Death Trio Traced To Chicago." On July 31, the paper trumpeted, "Capone's Gun Killed Yale, Says Informer."

The *Trib* and other papers reported that New York police commissioner Grover Whalen traveled to Chicago and gathered what he believed to be enough evidence to charge Capone with murder, but the Brooklyn grand jury failed to indict anyone for Yale's killing.

circa 1929

CHAPTER SIX

THE BEGINNING OF THE END

———◆———

U nited States attorney George E. Q. Johnson and IRS special agent Frank Wilson knew that Capone's return to Chicago would further intensify the cycle of gang violence and distract him from paying attention to the details of his multimillion-dollar operations. Clearly a successful prosecution of Capone required enormous diligence and a tedious survey of financial transactions, but the two were encouraged by the fact that Al had begun to lose control over his empire. First, the pineapple primary damaged his political faction at city hall; second, the newspapers unraveled the sham transactions surrounding his Miami house; and third, the New York police almost nailed him for the murder of Frankie Yale.

Guided by Johnson's interpretations of the tax evasion laws and the 1927 Supreme Court ruling, Wilson had to find evidence that Capone earned at least $5,000 in undeclared income each year. Though Wilson and his team knew how to trace Capone's expenditures, they could not prove how the money came into his pocket. The biggest gangster in Chicago was "completely anonymous when it came to income," Wilson declared. "He did all his business through front men or third parties. To discourage meddlers, his production department was turning out 50 corpses a year."

In their first step to bringing a tax evasion prosecution, Johnson and Wilson won the indictment of Frankie Lake and Terry Druggan, accusing the gold coast businessmen of hiding illicit beer profits. Though the arrests received a moment of notoriety in 1928, federal authorities were content to remain in the background, quietly gathering information about the fiscal deceptions needed to operate a $100 million per year bootleg and vice empire. As Capone returned to Chicago, the feds dispatched their agents to Miami, where they successfully interviewed Parker Henderson Jr. and Mayor Lummus, who explained how money from Chicago was wire-transferred to Florida. By the autumn of 1928, IRS special agent Charles Clarke had completed a thorough check of the records surrounding the Palm Island house.

"I have been able to secure from the Miami Beach Bank and Trust a list of all monies received by Capone which passed through that bank," Clarke wrote to the chief of the IRS Special Intelligence Unit, Elmer Irey. After searching through hundreds and hundreds of transactions handled by other parties, Clarke found "a $1,500 Western Union draft payable to and endorsed by Capone and [he] wanted large bills."

For the first time, federal agents found a transaction that could be directly traced to Capone. As Clarke's search confirmed, Capone dispatched a variety of flunkies who would use a ghost bank account to draw money, change a check, or hold property. Once the gofer had secured the amount, he turned it over to one of Capone's lieutenants, who then passed the bundle to Guzik or another close associate. In a hand-to-hand exchange, money was distributed.

The Miami sequences started to illuminate for Johnson and Wilson how Capone received and spent cash. From merchants and storekeepers, the feds learned that Al dropped $26,000 on chairs, sofas, rugs, and tables for use at his Prairie Avenue and Palm Island homes. Jewelers sold him $20,000 worth of silverware and thirty diamond-studded belt buckles, which Capone gave away as a sign of friendship. The list went on. To fully develop the evidence of tax evasion and fraud, Johnson and Wilson tried to match the known expenditures with wire transfers and the comings and goings of various fronts. The trail grew cold, however, because the feds could not find anyone who directly gave money to Capone as the result of a bootlegging transaction. They could not prove he earned the money that he had spent—nor could they prove that it actually belonged to Capone.

When Capone returned to Chicago in August 1928, Johnson and Wilson realized that their investigation would need an undercover agent and inside source. As Capone changed his headquarters from the Hotel Metropole to the grander Hotel Lexington down the street, the feds began a multifaceted strategy aimed at penetrating the underworld and documenting its financial operations. Johnson hired Eliot Ness. A college-educated man who had worked as a credit investigator, Ness was teamed with veteran Prohibition agent Dan Koken and sent to Chicago Heights, where they masqueraded as out-of-town bootleggers seeking to carve out a piece of midwestern territory. At the same time, other newly hired Prohibition agents and special IRS agents disguised themselves as hoods and fanned out into Capone's empire. While Ness, Koken, and others worked on the suburban fringes, Wilson scouted the possibility of landing a man right next to Capone inside the Lexington.

As Johnson and Wilson expected, Capone could not extricate himself from the feuds and conflicts that swirled around the underworld, especially since his repeated use of violence had triggered many of these vendettas. The feds wanted the violence to fester in the hope that the bloodletting would open the organization to the possibility of being infiltrated. Sure enough, with Capone resettled in Chicago, the long-simmering conflict over Tony Lombardo's reign at the Unione Sicilione heated up. When Capone and Lombardo had won the Unione's leadership in 1927 by besting the forces allied with Joey Aiello and his brothers, their victory drove the opposition to exile on the East Coast. From New Jersey, the Aiellos quietly climbed back into the bootlegging racket and positioned themselves to challenge the Unione leadership. Their original plan called for them to come out with Yale's blessing, but Frankie's untimely death prompted them to seek revenge.

Eluding Capone's detection, the brothers returned to Chicago and began to stalk Lombardo. On the afternoon of September 7, north side businessman Peter Rizzito called Lombardo at his office and kept him on the phone between 4:15 and 4:30 P.M. Although some gangsters were unsure if the call was a deliberate attempt to set up the kill, they and the cops had no doubt about what happened next: After Lombardo left the building at 8 South Dearborn, he turned onto Madison Street with his bodyguards, Joseph Ferraro and Joseph Lolordo, brother of Unione official Pasquale. In a crowd of shoppers and office workers, four shots rang out. Lombardo fell to the sidewalk, a portion of his head blown off. Ferraro also fell, mortally wounded. As the gunmen ran in opposite directions, Lolordo drew his pistol and chased one. A patrolman cut Lolordo off and disarmed him while the killers got away.

A week later, Rizzito was killed while standing in front of his Milton Street store. Police and reporters speculated that Capone had ordered the hit as retribution for setting up Lombardo. Two days later, Tony Aiello and one of his torpedoes were wounded in a machine-gun attack. The shootings enhanced Capone's ability to engineer the appointment of Pasquale Lolordo as Unione Sicilione chief. Over the next three and a half months, four Aiello triggermen and two Capone sluggers would die. During one shootout, north side goons cornered Jack McGurn in the lobby of a Rush Street hotel. As they opened fire, McGurn dropped into the phone booth, but his wounds weren't fatal.

As the violence continued, many of Chicago's reformers and blueblooded Republicans worried that gangs would take to the streets on Election Day and expand upon the hooliganism that made the pineapple primary an international event. They were determined to have a fair contest that would give their candidate, John Swanson, a chance to win the state's attorney position, so the reform faction enlisted the help of Frank Loesch, the chairman of the Chicago Crime Commission, to negotiate with Capone and arrange for a peaceful Tuesday. A fair election was the only way to oust these corrupt men, and Loesch faced up to a Faustian bargain: He would meet Capone and make a direct request for peace. To the petitioner's surprise, Capone agreed to keep his henchmen off the streets, but only in return for some protection.

When Election Day came and went, the authorities were astounded at the absence of the sluggers and goons who usually intimidated voters and ghosted ballots. In a first for the city, there were no complaints of fraud or violence.

Swanson and the reformers won the state's attorney's office, but Loesch had bargained away the prosecutor's ability to go after the man the Crime Commission identified as "Public Enemy Number 1."

Believing that he had neutralized the latest threat to his organization, Capone neglected the work of federal agents Ness and Koken, who uncovered a network of suburban bootleggers working in Chicago Heights. Though Ness openly curried favor with headline writers and newspaper photographers, Capone was aware that the feds weren't even close to the center of underworld power.

Picking up on the work of the feds, Chicago Heights police chief Leroy Gilbert collared two stragglers who had the misfortune of catching a few cases of surplus hooch. When he turned the men over to federal authorities, Gilbert told the prosecutors that he would testify in front of a grand jury scheduled for December 7, 1928. But on the night before his scheduled appearance, two shotgun blasts killed the chief while he sat in his living room reading the newspaper. Even though there was no evidence to suggest that Capone had ordered or authorized the hit, U.S. Attorney Johnson intended to make sure that he was held accountable.

Capone boarded a train for Miami, unaware of the prosecutor's intent, and believing that the authorities would not make a move against him. While Al celebrated in Florida, Johnson assembled a team of 100 agents and local cops. On the twelfth day of Christmas, January 6, 1929, a caravan of darkened cars rolled into Chicago Heights, stopping at the police station where a brigade of shotgun-wielding agents rushed into the building. After these good cops evicted the corrupt officers, they rounded up bootleggers, ransacked speakeasies, and raided the homes of known Capone associates. At the mansion that belonged to

A 1930 mug shot taken by the Miami Police Department.

Oliver Ellis—believed to be the shareholder fronting for Capone in a slot machine operation—they discovered a series of ledgers that revealed accounts at Pinkert State Bank in Cicero.

As word of the raids filtered south to Capone, the twists of underworld feuding prevented him from fully assessing the damage inflicted by Johnson's raiders. On the night of January 8, 1929—less than forty-eight hours after the feds had flexed their muscle—Mrs. Pasquale Lolordo admitted three men into her Chicago home and offered them drinks in the living room. As she prepared the refreshments, her husband entered the room and gunfire rang out. He died instantly; Mrs. Lolordo refused to identify the killers.

Days after the Lolordo killing, Jack McGurn boarded a train for Florida. Al still believed his biggest problems came from the north side gang of Bugs Moran and a few loyalists who were seeking to avenge the 1924 murder of Babyface O'Banion. McGurn convinced Capone that now was the time to finally end the feud and hopefully wipe out the competition.

As the triggerman returned north, Capone worked to cement his alibi. Dade County solicitor Robert Taylor asked Capone to come in for an interview about his real estate dealings and cash transactions, and they agreed to meet the morning of February 14. In the meantime, McGurn hatched a plan to lure Moran and his thugs into a trap. Killers, masquerading as cops, would enter Moran headquarters at the SMC Cartage Company, and kill their prey inside. To spring this deadly gambit, McGurn would provide Moran and his crew with a shipment of first-rate liquor, then use the gunmen dressed as cops to stage a raid.

To carry out the assassination, McGurn called on Fred "Killer" Burke, a Capone associate who worked out of St. Louis. On top of rum-running activities, Burke was an accomplished stickup man, and his face was posted for bank robberies in four states. Another crew member was Joseph Lolordo, who sought vengeance for the killing of his brother, Pasquale. Promised $1,000 apiece, veteran Capone gunners John Scalise and Albert Anselmi signed up. McGurn also recruited Harry and Phil Keywell, hard guys from Detroit's Purple Gang, for extra protection. To secure the stretch of Clark Street in front of the SMC garage, the Keywells rented an apartment across the street.

The plan took off when McGurn finally hired Claude Maddox to hot-wire a police car and grab a few extra uniforms. Then, Machine Gun McGurn arranged for a freelance booze hijacker to dangle a shipment of Old Log Cabin, bonded Canadian whiskey, in front of Moran. When the first delivery was completed, McGurn's middleman offered another. Insisting that the goods were taken "right off the river" that ran between Ontario and Michigan, the broker agreed to a cut-rate price of $57 per case. Moran jumped at the terms and set the delivery for 10:30 A.M. on the morning of St. Valentine's Day.

After the deal was set, McGurn and his girlfriend, Louise Rolfe, checked into the Stevens Hotel—a deliberate attempt to establish an alibi. As the morning broke to a temperature of eighteen degrees, the Keywells posted their lookout. Shortly before ten-thirty, the brothers saw a man pull up to the SMC Cartage Company garage, step out of his car, and enter. Within a few minutes, Burke, Anselmi, Scalise, and Lolordo arrived in a black-and-white police car. The four men rushed out of their car, two wearing long overcoats and two in police uniforms. They walked into the storefront and immediately found their way to the unheated garage in back, where seven men with several thousand dollars in each of their pockets awaited the delivery of booze. Except for a German shepherd guard dog tied to a pipe, they looked like a group of investors eyeing a potential piece of property.

Though Frank and Pete Gusenberg were experienced trig-germen for Moran, they bought the ruse and willingly handed over their weapons, obeying the cardinal rule of never shooting at cops. Safecracker John May, saloonkeeper Albert Weinshank, Moran's brother-in-law Albert Kashellek, and gang bookkeeper Adam Heyer also fell for the disguises and didn't resist. The seventh man, optometrist Reinhard Schwimmer, didn't know what to do—he enjoyed the company of hoods but had never expected to be rounded up. Moran, however, was not there.

After a cursory frisk, the four opened fire with two machine guns and two sawed-off shotguns. Six people died within a minute, each sustaining more than a dozen wounds in the back. Only Frank Gusenberg was left alive, writhing on the floor.

Sergeant Clarence Sweeney was the first real cop to arrive on the scene, and he questioned Gusenberg. Asked to identify the gunmen, the dying thug answered, "Nobody shot me."

The St. Valentine's Day Massacre.

Having known Gusenberg since their high school days, Sweeney pressed again and again, but received no reply. Before the gangster died, Sweeney asked, "Want a preacher, Frank?"

"No," Gusenberg said. "I'm cold."

At the same time, Capone calmly sat before a court stenographer in Miami, fielding the questions posed to him by the Dade County solicitor Taylor. While Capone established an ironclad alibi, the interview provided authorities with their first admission that Capone actually received the cash wired from Chicago. According to Capone, he considered the money to be income from his constant betting. This self-incriminating statement proved to be the first piece of evidence that directly linked Capone to any kind of an income.

By late afternoon, Capone had returned to his Palm Island house, where he learned that the attackers had failed to kill Moran. Figuring that cops were rounding up his gang, Moran and his associates had never gone inside, instead heading north on Clark Street.

His gang had killed the wrong men.

❖ ❖ ❖

"This is what we do to traitors."

At first, Capone believed he could stare down the international notoriety surrounding the massacre on St. Valentine's Day. By maintaining a high profile in Miami and holding parties that would lead up to the Jack Sharkey–Young Stribling heavyweight championship bout, Al portrayed himself as having nothing to hide—an attitude intended to bolster his claim of innocence. But the papers, the reformers, and his rivals were too eager to blame him for the carnage. Outraged at the gruesome executions, the Chamber of Commerce and other Chicago civic organizations posted a $50,000 reward for information leading to the arrest and conviction of the triggermen. Around the world, headline writers used the killings to depict Chicago as a modern-day Sodom gripped by the collusion of Capone-led gangsters and corrupt pols. In the face of this pressure, even Al's puppets—Mayor Big Bill Thompson and Police Chief William Russell—had to appear determined to track down and prosecute the dastardly killers.

Though coroners' juries, grand juries, cops, and prosecutors offered rounds and rounds of speculation that pointed to Capone and his men, they failed to produce any solid leads. At one point, the spotlight fixed on Al because Bugs Moran met with reporters and claimed that "only Capone kills like that."

A few days later, the headlines flip-flopped when Capone summoned reporters to Palm Island and turned the tables. "Only Bugs kills like that," he insisted, besting Moran by volunteering to give police a statement that fingered Moran. The posturing made for great copy and it continued to embarrass Chicago's police, who had begun to stitch together a circumstantial case against Machine Gun McGurn.

One of the first posed portraits of Al Capone.

But the mastermind of the killings remained one step ahead of the law. When the cops arrested him on murder charges arising out of the massacre, Louise Rolfe stepped forward to provide what became known as "the blonde alibi." Citing hotel records of their romantic night and early morning of intimacy, Rolfe easily (and accurately) accounted for McGurn's whereabouts on St. Valentine's Day. Within a week of his arrest, the case started to fall apart; eventually all charges were dismissed.

Despite his confidence that he could avoid prosecution or any formal implication for the murders, Capone began to see that the failure to kill Moran was turning into a colossal blunder. Stuck with the glare of publicity and the heightened police scrutiny, Capone found it almost impossible to keep a low profile.

As Capone tended to these problems, he remained unaware of the progress made by Johnson and the team of IRS special agents led by Frank Wilson: They began to uncover a series of Cicero bank accounts and aliases that could be directly traced to Ralph Capone. From the ledgers that were taken in the raid after the killing of Chicago Heights police chief Leroy Gilbert, IRS special agent Nils Tessem found a June 27, 1928, check for $2,130 signed by Ralph. In working this check through the Pinkert State Bank, the IRS began to document false names, dummy accounts, and a series of transactions that would total more than $1.8 million in unreported income. To Tessem's surprise, the scam was unmasked when he noticed that most of the deposits were divisible by $55—the Capone organization's price for a barrel of bootleg beer.

Faced with mounting pressure to take some form of public action against Capone, Johnson opted for a gamble: He issued a subpoena for Capone to appear before a grand jury on March 12,

1929. Concerned that such a move might tip off Capone to the imminent indictment of his brothers, Johnson gave reporters the impression that the heat would be focused on Al himself.

Inadvertently playing into the feds' trap, Capone tried to dodge the appearance, a move that once again monopolized the front page and diverted his attention from the real threat. To avoid testifying, Capone sent a letter from a Miami physician who claimed Capone was suffering from "bronco-pneumonia pleurisy." It was an obvious falsehood; the letter became the subject of a federal effort to prove that Capone deliberately ducked the subpoena and could therefore be found in contempt of court. As agents easily documented his comings and goings at Hialeah Racetrack, his parties at Palm Island, his frequent appearances with boxers Jack Sharkey and Jack Dempsey, Johnson pressed for another subpoena, which was issued.

Again, Capone misunderstood his antagonists. "They say the police of Chicago want to see me about the gang massacre," he told reporters in early March.

In mid-March, Johnson and Capone's lawyers reached a simple deal: Al would testify in front of the grand jury provided the panel did not ask about the St. Valentine's Day killings. Eager to question Capone about financial transactions, the feds arranged for a March 19 grand jury session that would last less than an hour. When he was quizzed about the twists and turns of checks and wire transfers, Capone conceded that he might have neglected to pay income tax. As he explained to a throng of scribes gathered outside the courthouse, he wanted to "split the difference" to clear up what appeared to be a minor matter. Capone pointed out that his tax settlement "might pay the salary of several Prohibition agents for a year or two."

Despite Johnson's threat, Capone allowed himself to become mired in yet another round of gangster intrigue. He learned that the present Unione Sicilione chief, Joseph "Hop Toad" Giunita, had formed an alliance with Joey Aiello. To compound this betrayal, Capone heard rumors that triggermen Albert Anselmi and John Scalise had joined the entente and had begun plotting an underworld coup.

Aware that this group could easily penetrate his inner circle and kill him, Capone quickly moved to test the loyalty of Anselmi and Scalise. At the end of April, Capone and one of his most trusted bodyguards, Frankie Rio, agreed to a ruse: In the presence of Anselmi and Scalise, the boss and his underling staged a heated argument that climaxed in a shouting match. As Capone feigned anger, Rio reached across the table and slapped the boss, then stormed out of the room. Stunned by the sequence, Anselmi and Scalise contacted Rio the next day and attempted to recruit him for their move against Capone. As these discussions continued, Rio secretly informed Al, who began laying plans to spring his own ambush.

He arranged for an elaborate dinner to take place on May 7 in a Hammond, Indiana roadhouse that he controlled. Capone invited more than 100 members of his organization, including Anselmi, Giunita, and Scalise. Casting the gathering as a celebration of success and loyal service, Al presided over a feast that produced plates and plates of pasta washed down by gallons of wine, liquor, and brandy. After the guests had completely relaxed, Capone dramatically redirected their attention, launching into a long speech about the need to root out betrayal and enforce the code of loyalty. Fingering Anselmi, Giunita, and Scalise, the boss identified them as disloyal. Henchmen sprang from the wings to bind them. Within a minute, Capone began to beat them with a baseball bat.

"This is what we do to traitors," Capone told his guests.

"When the men fell to the floor," noted Dr. Eli Jones, coroner of Lake County, Indiana, "their assailants stood over them and fired several shots in their backs."

A day after the killings made front-page news across the country, Capone, McGurn, Rio, and Guzik boarded a train heading east out of Chicago. Ostensibly traveling to Atlantic City to watch a fight, these men were going to the boardwalk to meet gangsters from around the country. Organized with the blessing of Little John Torrio, the meeting was the first effort to establish a national commission to mediate disputes among crime bosses. Capone felt ensnared in the cycle of violence that swirled around the St. Valentine's Day massacre, the Unione Sicilione leadership, and other feuds, and he looked to the gathering and Torrio as producing a possible vehicle for underworld peace.

❧ ❧ ❧

"I am a hustler."

So did the other attendees. To Capone's surprise, he was quite unpopular with his peers, who believed his organization had descended into an endless series of blood feuds and investigations.

Throughout the three-day summit from May 13 through May 16, Capone chafed at the open criticism of him, his organization, and his ways of transacting business. He tried to cast the dissatisfaction as the product of jealous rivals, and finally won a round when he prompted the other bosses to incorporate Max Annenberg's racing wire as the standard for bookmakers who took action on horses. But the crime bosses from Cleveland, Newark, and New York forced Capone to make a number of concessions. First, he had to swear off violence as a means of resolving disputes and submit all conflicting claims to a commission chaired by Torrio; second, he would have to accept his sworn rival, Joseph Aiello, as head of Chicago's Unione Sicilione; third, he would have to relinquish control of several gambling dens, including the Ship—the largest casino in Cicero.

These terms were designed to insult Capone, and he turned to Torrio as a possible ally. But the mild-mannered mobster, the man who always preferred compromise over conflict, refused to stand up for his former protégé. "There are two ways to power," Little John reportedly told the gathering. "Capone can rule for a while by blood and terror, but there will always be some who fight him with weapons. On the other hand, the man who can make money, big money, for others will eventually be regarded as indispensable."

Devastated by this rejection, Capone saw that his authority was being undermined and devalued. He also recognized that Torrio's rebuke would be perceived as an invitation to an assassin. He had arrived in Atlantic City hoping for triumph; he left in defeat, scared that any gangland rival could order his execution.

"Al's rise was meteoric and his fall equally swift," recalled his friend Jack Woodford, ". . . which testified somewhat to the accidental nature of it."

In dire need of a safe haven, Capone borrowed a move from Torrio, who four years earlier had escaped assassination attempts by opting for jail instead of the streets. On the last night of the Atlantic City gathering, May 16, Capone telephoned two Philadelphia detectives he had come to know through his connections to boxer Jack Sharkey. Tipping off James "Shooey" Malone and John Creedon to his travel plans, Capone arranged to have himself arrested. He was to appear on May 17 at a downtown Philly movie theater, where Malone and Creedon would confront him and discover a loaded .38-caliber revolver on his person. He would be charged with carrying a concealed weapon. Then, Capone and his bodyguard Frankie Rio would be whisked downtown and indicted by a grand jury within a day, and would plead guilty in exchange for a one-year prison term to begin immediately. Capone expected to be out after eight months.

On the morning of May 17, Capone and Rio hopped the Short Line to the City of Brotherly Love. At the agreed-upon time and place, they were confronted by Malone and Creedon. As the detectives found Capone's gun and formally notified him of his arrest, the gangster slipped a roll of two hundred $100 bills into Malone's hands. With $20,000 to split, Malone and Creedon stuck to the script. A day after his arrest, Capone had become inmate 90725.

At Eastern Penitentiary, Capone was quickly moved into a section known as Park Avenue, where he enjoyed a carpeted and furnished cell. Through the bars, he granted interviews to reporters, claiming that the Atlantic City conference was an unqualified success. Capone served as library file-card clerk, a job that gave him the opportunity to brush up on his reading. When one scribe asked about his book list, Capone mentioned his dabblings in European history and gave a short lecture on Napoléon.

As Capone found safety in his custom cell, George Johnson and Special Agent Frank Wilson took the next step toward prosecuting him for income tax evasion. Throughout July, August, and September, the feds meticulously retraced the money trail through the Pinkert State Bank, showing a grand jury how Ralph Capone used fake accounts to conceal deposit after deposit after deposit. Successfully winning the testimony of bank personnel who described the messengers and gofers making these transactions, Wilson and special agents Nils Tessem and Archie Martin detailed how Ralph controlled accounts in the fictitious names of James Carroll, James Costello Jr., James Carson, Harry Roberts, and Harry White. "In none of the investigations," Tessem wrote, "has any evidence been produced tending to show that Ralph J. Capone has been engaged in a legitimate business, unless it can be said that horse racing in some states is a legitimate business." In the first week of October, the grand jury voted for a sealed seven-count indictment. Ralph was apprehended October 8, ringside at a boxing match.

With Al Capone in jail and Ralph facing trial, the feds picked up their pace. Receiving additional manpower from Washington, Special Agent Frank Wilson, his boss Elmer Irey, and the U.S. Attorney Johnson used the early months of 1930 to launch their effort to infiltrate the highest levels of the Capone organization. As the reams of ledgers and bank records showed, both Capone brothers relied on a long string of intermediaries to handle cash, divide it into shares, and then distribute the bundles.

As Wilson's crew worked the paper trail, Prohibition agents Eliot Ness and his partner, Paul Robsky, experimented with the new technique of climbing up a telephone pole, cutting into the wire, and using alligator clips to intercept conversations. With one station posted near Ralph's headquarters at the Montmartre Café in Cicero and others shuffled around Chicago, Ness and Robsky tracked a number of booze and beer shipments and conducted a highly publicized series of raids. Though Ness's campaign had little to do with IRS efforts to find evidence of tax evasion, the frequent hauls of liquor and beer effectively served to divert Capone from the investigation's real threat.

Despite the reputation of the "untouchables" as cops beyond bribery or graft, the Capones managed to learn of the squad's ability to tap phones. Consequently, Ralph and Al developed a code for their conversations between the Pennsylvania prison and the Chicago area speakeasies. Concentrating on this effort to outwit the feds and their nuisance raids, the Capones were completely unaware that Tessem had traced a check endorsed by Frank Nitti to the Schiff Savings Bank, where owner Bruno Schiff showed the IRS a secret ledger that detailed $734,887.81 in deposits made on behalf of Nitti. Faced with the decision of being indicted or testifying against Nitti, Schiff became the first important insider to turn against the outfit and help the government.

On March 23, 1930, six days after Al Capone's release from prison and less than forty-eight hours after his return to Chicago, U.S. attorney Johnson announced the tax evasion indictment of Frank Nitti. Eighteen days later, the trial of Ralph Capone began.

Reporters and headline writers did their best to dramatize the proceedings, but the government showcased a strategy that perplexed many observers. Instead of accusing Ralph of bootlegging and pimping, gambling and extorting, the prosecutors relied on a tedious but thorough tour of bank records, deposit slips, withdrawal sheets, and teller testimonies. Disappointed by this dreary and monotonous presentation of the evidence, many of the reporters doubted the prosecution's ability to persuade jurors that Ralph had committed a felony, but the jury took only two and a half hours of deliberations to convict Ralph on all counts, after which he stood at the defense table shaking his head and telling his lawyers, "I don't understand this at all."

Al finally wised up. Hiring tax specialist Lawrence Mattingly out of Washington, D.C., Capone used this mouthpiece to approach the government and raise the possibility of negotiating a deal that would avoid prosecution. "Mr. Mattingly has called at the office of the Internal Revenue Agent in Charge on several occasions," wrote Special Agent Arthur Madden, two days after the end of Ralph's trial. "Evidently, he wants to reach a settlement."

Johnson would string Mattingly along, but he had no intention of striking a deal. Instead, he used Mattingly's statements as incriminating admissions against Capone. As Johnson continued these discussions, Wilson and his crew developed two new leads: First, they discovered that a minor mob lawyer named Edward "Artful Eddie" O'Hare might be willing to assist the feds in exchange for helping his son gain admission to the Naval Academy in Annapolis; second, they learned that a former cashier, Fred Ries, was willing to directly implicate Capone and Guzik in a series of transactions showing that these men had income from illegal activities.

As the feds went after these two new cracks in his organization, Capone made a mistake born of confusion. Instead of keeping a low profile and seeking to mend relations within his organization, he took to the streets and front pages, opening a downtown kitchen for the growing number of unemployed, homeless, and poor caught in the deepening economic depression. As he had once cast himself as an honest rogue and a defender of the little guy, Al tried to reinvent himself as a man of the people who was forced into a dishonest life. To mount this deception, Capone invited reporters to be with him as he traveled the streets, ostensibly overseeing the soup kitchen at 935 South State Street, a parlor that served thousands of meals per week. Though the newsmen fell for this ruse and provided

◆ GEORGE JOHNSON ◆

Fifty-four years old at the time of his appointment as United States attorney for the northern district of Illinois, George Emmerson Q. Johnson had already established himself as one of Chicago's premier lawyers. When he accepted the appointment from President Calvin Coolidge in February 1927, Johnson took a pay cut to $15,000, but he felt it was his civic duty to direct the federal government's efforts to prosecute the city's most ferocious gangsters.

Born to Swedish immigrants who farmed in Iowa and Wisconsin, Johnson had never bought into Chicago's cynical attitude toward the underworld: He worked his way through law school and solemnly believed in the heartland ethic that rewards hard work and fair play. With his thick mop of gray hair frequently flying off into a winglike coiffure, Johnson could easily be mistaken for a zealot who lacked humor and perspective. Though he eagerly stepped onto a soapbox to claim that hoods and racketeers are not a necessary evil of urban life, he also had a dash of homespun, self-deprecating wit: He frequently joked that his father needed to give him the initial Q as a means of dis-tinguishing a dim-witted boy from all the other George Johnsons running around the Midwest.

Known for his diligence, the pros-ecutor believed that he could suc-ceed where Chicago's corrupt police had openly failed. His first move was to assemble a team of incorruptible investigators; second, he immersed himself and each of his agents in a full-fledged study of Chicago's gangs, their memberships, turfs, and hierarchies. Recognizing that the police could not be trusted to gather such important information, the prosecutor delved into the libraries of the city's newspapers, amassing a clip and card file that became the first citywide official database of the rackets.

With his knowledge of how cer-tain activies interlocked and over-lapped, Johnson was the first prosecutor to attack the gangsters as an enterprise. "Organized crime was a business," he said. "Al Capone could have been a brilliant busi-nessman. . . . He had the organiza-tional ability, cunning, intellect and street smarts it took to succeed."

To crack open this illicit network of graft, booze, and violence, Johnson launched a methodical investigation that worked its way up the ladder of authority. While Capone remained his target, Johnson directed his agents to use their powers against dozens of small-time hoods who could piece together a picture of how gangsters earned, invested, and spent their millions. He was the first prosecutor to understand that the biggest crooks forgo stickups for semi-legitimate businesses.

As his team of agents and assistant U.S. attorneys began to unravel Capone's web of deceit and corruption, Johnson stepped back from the particulars of the probe, devoting his energy to the administrative and bureaucratic infighting between the Internal Revenue Service and the newly created Federal Bureau of Investigation, headed by J. Edgar Hoover, brother of the newly elected president. While Andrew Mellon's Treasury Department, with its IRS and Bureau of Alcohol, Tobacco, and Firearms, stood squarely behind Johnson's effort to make a tax evasion prosecution against many of the hoodlums, Hoover balked, trying to maneuver the FBI into a larger role.

This tug-of-war reached its climax in 1931 when Hoover deliberately withdrew FBI assistance from the effort to prosecute Capone. When a sheaf of Chicago newspaper clippings came across Hoover's desk and he saw that Johnson's office had received credit for the indictment of Capone, the director scribbled in a note, "Well of all the bunk . . . now he [Johnson] basks in the sunlight of the effort which he did everything to avoid."

Years later, Hoover would be one of the first to cite Capone's conviction as proof of the FBI's ability to battle organized crime. As Hoover's revisionist tales became accepted as popular history, Johnson went on to serve as a federal judge and then left the bench for a lucrative law practice. Unlike so many others who claimed credit for busting Capone, Johnson refused to cash in. He never wrote articles or books explaining how he directed the probe that captured the original Public Enemy Number 1. Others would shamelessly exaggerate their importance, but Johnson retained his dignity, remaining humble and soft-spoken about the biggest case of his life.

a number of full-page feature spreads, they never found out that a great deal of the food was "donated" by restaurants, meat packers, bakers, and grocers' associations organized through Maxie Eisen, one of Capone's best labor sluggers and union extortionists.

Capone went so far as to present himself as a twisted amalgam of Robin Hood and Karl Marx. "The men with power are the men with money or the will to take it. They break down into two classes: The squares and the hustlers. I am a hustler, but I got respect for squares," he said. Noting that a self-made capitalist—an entrepreneur like Henry Ford or Thomas Edison—could be seen as "a guy with brains and determination and willingness to work for what he wants," Capone claimed that he could easily understand and respect men of such caliber.

Capone figured his soup kitchen and publicity program, coupled with bribery and graft, would give him access to a wide variety of ward-based political organizations that could reestablish his hold on the city. But the depression and Mayor Big Bill Thompson's repeated abuses had pushed the situation beyond the gangster's reach: The city administration spent $23 million more than it collected; teachers, firemen, and cops were laid off; private donations were used to finance public schools.

"He got put away in Pennsylvania for 10 months," said Capone's friend Jack Woodford. "When he came out, it was to face a whole new world."

Capone continued to behave as if he were at the peak of his reign. While he now understood that the feds were after his financial information and working overtime to make a tax case, he continued to indulge himself in a number of spectacles to create the illusion that he still held power.

Though the gangsters knew he was losing his grip on the

rackets, national magazines and publishing houses had just begun to catch up. Reporter Edward Dean Sullivan published a serious study, *Rattling the Cop on Chicago Crime*; Fawcett Publications produced fifty-cent picture books like *The Inside Story of Chicago's Master Criminal*. Such national magazines as the *New Yorker*, *North American Review*, *Collier's*, and the *Nation* commissioned lengthy essays about his rule and personality. *True Crime* and *Master Detective* filled their pages with lore of his escapades and alleged rubouts. *Chicago Tribune* reporter Fred Pasley published *Al Capone: The Biography of a Self-Made Man*. And then Hollywood began cranking out a series of gangster films, starting with *Doorway to Hell*, featuring Lew Ayres as the Florida-based boss Louis Ricarno, *Public Enemy* with James Cagney, and *Little Caesar*, with Edward G. Robinson. Onetime Chicago newsman Ben Hecht turned his screenwriting talents to *Scarface*, starring Paul Muni. Capone saw this highbrow activity as proof that he was on the track to regaining his grip.

Adding to the hype was the attention of the foreign press: *Le Journal de Paris* sent their crime reporter for an interview. The Viennese newspapers editorialized on Chicago's government and its relationship to the underworld. Fleet Street carried a special dispatch about how Capone hosted British heavyweight Bob Fitzsimmons at the American Derby in Washington Park.

The extravaganzas made it easy for the thirty-one-year-old hoodlum to lose his concentration and focus. While one Capone biographer, Laurence Bergreen, attributes the loss of mental agility to latent syphilis, many others view the decline as the result of an immature man finally reaching the limits of his skills and intelligence. By 1930, Capone could no longer slug his way to the top; gangland killings and betrayals were useless in a society soon to repeal Prohibition. Instead of adapting to these changes, a bewildered Capone retreated into his own shortcomings, returning to the boy who had never moved past the destruction of his shoe-shine stand.

Only violence would force Capone to pay attention to the poor state of his business.

A murder on May 31, 1930, appeared to be another hit in an endless squabble over who delivered beer to a particular part of the city's north side. While it received a prominent display in the papers, Capone and his lieutenants considered it as just another beef among the truckers who were hired by speakeasies and saloons to keep the regular supply in Bugs Moran's territory. When a similar killing occurred on the next day, gangland started to ask questions, only to get conflicting answers. On the third day came a third murder, and Capone realized that his rival, Moran, and a group of haulers were unable to resolve their disputes. By the fourth day, another body surfaced; it was then that Capone learned his longtime pal, associate, and employee, Alfred "Jake" Lingle, was negotiating a deal with Moran. According to one report, Lingle was using his influence to broker a bribe that would allow Bugs and Julius "Potatoes" Kaufman to reopen their gambling club on Waveland Avenue, in the shadow of Wrigley Field. Using his friendship with Police Chief William Russell, Lingle demanded that Moran and Kaufman offer him a fee to make sure the club opened on June 9 without police interference.

As one gangland murder washed up each day in the first week of June, Capone saw that Lingle might be using his position to play rival gangsters against each other. Since Russell had taken office in 1928, Lingle had served as a crucial emissary between the cops and Capone, but by the summer of 1930 he had begun to double-cross Al, by dealing with Moran. Capone also suspected that Lingle was about to sell out to the feds.

Around noon on June 9, Lingle left his suite at the Stevens Hotel and walked down Michigan Avenue to his office at the Tribune tower. By 1 P.M. he was on his way to the Illinois Central Station on Randolph, where he planned to take the race-day special to Washington Park. Stopping at the Hotel Sherman to buy coffee, Lingle ran into Police Sergeant Tom Alcock. "I'm being tailed," Lingle told the cop.

At the newsstand in front of the Public Library, Lingle bought the *Racing Forum* and lit a cigar. Studying the tables for other races, Lingle walked into the Illinois Central Station, to the east ramp of the platform. More than a dozen people saw a blond man break through the crowd and pull out a revolver, bringing the barrel to within inches of Lingle's head. One shot blew into his skull.

The assailant fled.

Once again, Chicago's gangland murders became front-page news around the world. At first the *Tribune* and all the other papers depicted the killing as an outrageous assault on liberty, turning Lingle into a martyr, but Lingle's large public funeral was the first sign of the deceased's checkered history. When IRS Special Agent Frank Wilson saw this part of the spectacle, his suspicions were immediately aroused. Within days of the murder, Wilson had gathered enough information to uncover the mystery of Lingle's double life.

Surely a series of newspaper stories about a crooked reporter could further damage Capone and possibly shake loose a few more potential informers, so Wilson met with John Rogers of the *St. Louis Post-Dispatch* and provided details of the corrupt relationship between Capone and Lingle. Eager to embarrass its midwestern rival, the *Post-Dispatch* pressed ahead and published details that sent a battle-hardened public into a state of shock. As the revelations forced the resignation of Police Chief Russell, the *Tribune* backpedaled, denouncing the man who was martyred and lionized. Newspapers tripped over each other to humble publisher Col. Robert R. McCormick and discredit the *Tribune*, and Capone found himself unable to manipulate the scribes. With Lingle gone, Capone lost a crucial method of projecting the perception of his power.

Though a new police chief would devote months to eventually making an arrest in the Lingle case, the feds reaped immediate results. First, the sensational headlines helped Wilson persuade former Capone cashier Fred Ries to testify against the Big Fella. Johnson and Wilson kept Ries under guard and even offered to send him to South America in an effort to guarantee his safety. He was their first witness who could tell a grand jury that Al Capone and Jack Guzik personally directed and received proceeds from dummy accounts, fake check cashings, and wire transfers.

Chicago Cubs great Gabby Hartnett autographs a baseball for Al Capone Jr. at Wrigley Field.

Second, Rogers's success in breaking the Lingle story encouraged attorney Artful Eddie O'Hare to seek a deal with the feds. With Rogers acting as an intermediary, O'Hare met Wilson and offered his services as a government informant, agreeing to help the IRS trace the millions siphoned through Capone's gaming operations. (Many years later, Chicago authorities would name their airport after O'Hare's son.) While Ries provided the critical link of putting cash in Capone's and Guzik's hands, O'Hare unlocked the interlocking dummy accounts and aliases that served as holding bins.

On September 18, 1930, Ries testified in front of the federal grand jury that indicted Guzik for tax evasion. Instead of heeding this obvious warning, Capone once again turned to the streets, looking for a big score that could overshadow the string of defeats he had recently suffered. By early October, his triggermen had traced longtime rival Joey Aiello to a bungalow on Kolmar Street in the city's west side. Renting the apartment across the street, the torpedoes drew their bead on the night of October 23. Two bursts of machine-gun fire ripped into his body, and Aiello became the seventh president of the Unione Sicilione to die in office.

For Capone, the triumph of eliminating a rival was shortlived. Within three weeks of Aiello's death, a jury convicted Guzik of tax evasion. By the end of December, Frank Nitti had pleaded guilty and received an eighteen-month sentence in exchange for his cooperation with government agents.

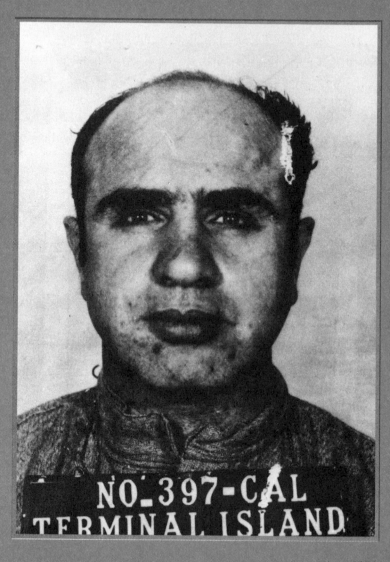

NO. 397-CAL
TERMINAL ISLAND

circa 1939

CHAPTER SEVEN

THE FALL

———◆———

As Capone emerged from another round of gang violence, IRS special agent Frank Wilson made the final breakthrough. Unlike the other clues that came from intrigue and informers, double-crossers and frightened flunkies, this piece of evidence was wedged between the bundles of papers and files closeted in his basement office. During the time that Wilson and his crew had sifted through more than 1,700,000 items, they had apparently overlooked a bundle of ledgers taken in one of the police raids following the 1926 murder of Assistant State's Attorney William McSwiggin. When Wilson finally stumbled upon these books, he found three black ledgers with red corners dated 1924–1926. As he reviewed the columns marked Bird Cage, 21, Craps, Faro, Roulette, Horse Bets, he saw disbursements for R, whom he believed to be Ralph Capone; J, whom he surmised was Jack Guzik; and A for Al Capone. Other categories included Town for bribes, Frank for Frankie

Pope, and Pete for Peter Penovich, the first manager of the Hawthorn Smoke Shop. On one corner, Wilson found the notation "Frank paid $17,500 for Al."

At the same time, the feds began to see dividends from their undercover work. Special Agent James Sullivan had quietly worked his way through Capone and Guzik's bordello operations, eyeing whores and pimps as potential informers. After a raid on the Harlem Inn, he came across a woman presumably in her fifties who had traveled her way through whorehouses across Chicago. Calling herself Reigh Count, after the winner of the 1928 Kentucky Derby, she agreed to snitch for $50 per week. Through Count, the feds were able to account for a continuous series of transactions that would identify Capone as the owner of an illicit business and therefore the recipient of income that should have been taxed.

A second undercover operative, Special Agent Mike Malone, had actually infiltrated the Hotel Lexington by masquerading as De Angelo, a hard guy from New York. Pretending to be running from a shooting flap, Malone succeeded in winning a room on the Lexington's seventh floor, next door to Capone's bodyguard Phil D'Andrea. Through Malone, the feds discovered that Capone was finally taking the IRS seriously and actually considered hiring five out-of-town gunmen to kill Wilson for $25,000. While Wilson easily dodged the threat, Malone also told Wilson that Capone would approach former assistant to the IRS commissioner Joseph Callan and offer a $1.5 million bribe to be passed on to the Special Intelligence Unit chief Elmer Irey. When the move was made, Callan and Irey rejected it.

As Capone grew desperate, the IRS stepped up its arduous effort to match the 1924–1926 ledger entries with deposit slips, wire transfers, and other financial transactions. When

Wilson pressed Fred Ries and Eddie O'Hare for answers about Capone's early operations in Cicero, the informers coughed up an important lead: The cashier at that time was Leslie Shumway, who now worked at a Miami dog track. The feds would have to find Shumway before the end of March 1931 to beat the five-year statute of limitations.

Within the week, Wilson found Shumway working as a cashier at the Biscayne Kennel Club. Though initially denying any knowledge of gambling in Cicero, Shumway quickly changed his mind after Wilson explained the options of jail, public exposure that could lead to a gangster's bullet, or protective custody. By the time Wilson and U.S. Attorney Johnson had properly questioned and prepared Shumway for his grand jury testimony in Chicago, authorities had less than a week to issue the indictment. A grand jury voted the first bill on March 13, and the court granted Johnson's request to seal it pending further inquiry.

By the time Johnson had impaneled a new grand jury in April, Capone and his lawyers, Thomas Nash and Michael Ahearn, had learned of the indictment. At the beginning of May, Nash and Ahearn approached Johnson with the possibility of a plea bargain. With Capone continuing to talk tough in public, his offer of a cash payment and jail time took the feds by surprise.

Rejecting the offer outright would risk losing the case at trial, Johnson figured. The prosecution was aware that Capone and his corps of corrupt cops, judges, and prosecutors could get to any Chicago jury, so he spent a great deal of time seriously entertaining the prospect of a deal. On the other hand, Johnson felt that only a public trial would totally humiliate Capone and hold him accountable for his crimes. When word of the secret negotiations came to U.S. district court judge James Wilkerson, the jurist summoned the prosecutor and

⬥ ELIOT NESS ⬥

THE "UNTOUCHABLE"
ELIOT NESS.

H e copped all the fame. Headlines, his own book, radio shows, a
television series, and movies trumpeted Eliot Ness as the good-looking, fast-talking G-man who took on
Al Capone and won.

For the real Eliot Ness, though,
the legends are a far cry from the
truth. Born to Norwegian parents in
north Chicago in 1903, Eliot King
had taken his mother's name by the
time he went through the University
of Chicago, from which he graduated
in the the top third of his class. His
good looks and quick wit always
attracted a crowd who enjoyed his
company. A tennis player, he moved

with the natural grace of an athlete.

His brother-in-law, Alexander
Jamie, was a cop who became one of
the first FBI agents. Ness wanted to
follow in his footsteps. After Jamie
taught him how to shoot a gun, Ness
left his job as an investigator for
insurance companies and joined the
Prohibition Bureau in 1928, where
he was hired by U.S. attorney
George E. Q. Johnson. Ness mastered the simplest details, staking
out speakeasies and raiding delivery
trucks. A good storyteller who
enjoyed puffing up his own importance, he frequently crossed paths
with reporters who would curry his
favor by giving him ink.

To Johnson and the others who
were intimately involved with the
effort to prosecute top-level gangsters, Ness's chatter to the papers
served an unusual purpose: By
speaking of his own exploits, Ness
steered reporters, gangsters, and the
public away from the important
details of sifting through financial
ledgers, bank accounts, and check
drafts. Johnson and the Internal
Revenue Service special agent Frank
Wilson actually encouraged Ness to
boast of his prowess in stopping the
delivery of beer and liquor.

Though Ness and his partner,

Neal Koken, provided an important tip during their undercover investigation in Chicago Heights, most of their notoriety came from raids that were designed to pressure small-time bootleggers. These operations barely dented the multimillion-dollar empire of booze and graft, but they were prime-time photo-ops splashed across the front page. By 1930, the legend of crime-busting Ness had taken hold.

When Capone was put away, Ness sought a transfer to the FBI, but director J. Edgar Hoover was reluctant to reward anyone who claimed to be connected with the prosecution of Public Enemy Number 1. Openly resenting Ness's fame and his ability to gain favorable press clippings, Hoover refused to hire him.

In 1935, Ness accepted a job as Cleveland's director of public safety, the prized appointee of reform mayor Harold Hitz Burton. Though he started out with a number of important initiatives, Ness soon fell prey to a long series of domestic and political squabbles. Quarreling with his political patrons, divorcing the first of his three wives, and wrestling with the entrenched bureaucracy of Cleveland's police force, Ness the Prohibition buster soon became known as Ness the barfly. His friend-

ships with reporters kept a number of drunken episodes out of the public domain, but Ness could not count on his cronies when his car spun out of control on a March night in 1942. He left the scene, only to be tracked down by his own cops.

During World War II, he tried Washington and New York, but yearned for another chance in Cleveland. In 1946, he mounted his comeback, seeking the Republican nomination for mayor. Once he qualified as the party's standard-bearer, Ness raised $150,000 and outspent his opponent by a 3-to-1 margin. Money was not the issue—he lost the election by a humiliating tally of 186,000 to 86,000.

His newspaper and publishing friends arranged for him to publish his memoirs, which exaggerated his importance and claimed part of the victory in prosecuting Capone, but Ness never recovered from his defeat in Cleveland. Despite his carefully crafted persona as the man who crusaded against Prohibition, he lived out his days as an alcoholic, shifting from one job to the next. He died in 1957.

clearly laid down his law: A plea bargain would not be accepted by the court. However, while leading Capone's defense to believe that a plea bargain was still possible, Johnson pushed the new grand jury for a second indictment. On June 5, 1931, the panel voted for a sixty-five-page, twenty-two-count listing of alleged income tax evasion and fraud dating from 1924 to 1929. According to the grand jury, Capone earned at least $1,035,654.84 in those years and neglected to pay $215,080.48.

A week later, Eliot Ness and his crew of Prohibition agents basked in the glory of a third Capone indictment. This time, the grand jury alleged more than 5,000 violations of the Volstead Act, dating to 1922 when Capone bought a used truck for John Torrio. In this indictment, 4,000 counts referred to specific deliveries of beer, and sixty-eight people were accused.

The newspapers that once had lionized Capone were the first to participate in his public whipping, while lawyers Nash and Ahearn once again pressed for a plea bargain. Despite Wilkerson's stubborn refusals, a deal emerged in mid-July: Capone would plead guilty to tax evasion, fraud, and Volstead Act violations in exchange for a two-and-a-half-year sentence. After negotiating the compromise, Johnson sought guidance from his superiors in Washington. On July 24, 1931, U.S. Attorney General William Mitchell wrote, "Your proposal to make a recommendation to the court as to the sentence to be imposed on Alphonse Capone has my approval."

In explaining his decision to accept the plea bargain, Mitchell also mentioned that the "immediate imprisonment" of Capone was of greater public interest than a contested trial.

As word of the plea bargain filtered out into the press, the scribes immediately saw the deal as Capone's capitulation. On the front pages of the Chicago dailies, reporters speculated

Capone poses with his lawyers during pre-trial hearings.

that the Big Fella would be in Leavenworth by Labor Day, and they carried a dispatch from Springfield, where President Herbert Hoover made a special mention of Johnson's victory in getting Capone to admit wrongdoing. When Capone appeared in front of Judge Wilkerson on July 30, he was ready to uphold his word.

With prosecutor Johnson and his team of agents looking on, defense lawyer Ahearn rose to address Wilkerson. Once he raised the subject of a guilty plea in exchange for a reduced sentence, the judge cut him off. "It is time," Wilkerson thundered, "for somebody to impress upon this defendant that it is utterly impossible to bargain with a federal court."

At the defense table, Capone's posture immediately changed: His hulking shoulders slumped and hunched forward, wrinkling the silk-and-linen fabric of his pea-green suit. Wilkerson's move forced him to plead not guilty, and a trial was set for October.

Though Damon Runyon and Meyer Berger were among the

dozens of scribes packed into Judge Wilkerson's court on October 7, the glitz of the crowd belied the tedium of the evidence. For the next seventeen days, legal maneuvers would dominate newspapers around the world, but reporters found themselves quickly lost in the minutiae of a prosecution based on wire transfers and checks, dummy accounts and aliases, bearded transactions and lavish spending for household items or clothes.

To further implicate Capone and cement his connection to income, the prosecution introduced evidence of tax lawyer Mattingly's offer to pay off Al's tax liability. In reading one of Mattingly's letters to the jury, prosecutors demonstrated that Capone knew that his income was liable for taxation.

After five days of prosecution testimony, the defense needed two days to mount a series of missteps. Trying to blame Capone's situation on his well-known habit of betting on losing horses, the defense team brought a chrous line of bookies to the witness stand. From Chicago wire men Oscar Gutter and Joe Yario to Hialeah hustler Budd Gentry, Capone was depicted as the unluckiest gambler of all, a hunch player who won on the single shot and lost on the parlay. To open laughter and outright anger from Wilkerson, the defense attempted to portray Capone as a misguided Robin Hood who threw his roll on the sport of kings.

When the jury began its deliberation on the afternoon of October 17, they needed less than nine hours to reach their verdict. They found Capone guilty on five counts—three felonies for evading taxes and two misdemeanors for failing to file an income tax return. Noting that he won acquittal on seventeen alleged offenses, Capone figured that he would pay a stiff fine and spend two to three years in jail.

Wilkerson, however, had another view. As a smiling Capone stood before him on October 24, the stern judge fashioned a total sentence of eleven years to begin immediately. "It was a smashing blow to the massive gang chief. He tried to take it with a smile," wrote Meyer Berger. "But that smile was almost pitiful. His clumsy fingers, tightly locked behind his back, twitched and twisted."

A moment of silence blanketed the courtroom before reporters broke for the exits to call their editors. The commotion triggered a chaotic outburst from the gallery, and Capone was immediately surrounded by marshals. He was given his hat and coat and then escorted to the elevator. Once the door closed and a moment of calm prevailed, the Big Fella stood next to the man he had known as De Angelo. IRS special agent Mike Malone revealed his true identity, and Capone saw that he had been played for a sucker.

"You look like a wop," Capone said. "You took your chances and I took mine."

Al Capone would spend eight years in various jails and prisons, shuttled between cells in Chicago, Atlanta, and Alcatraz, and hospital wards in Los Angeles and Lewisburg, Pennsylvania. In his first months of imprisonment, he had the run of Cook County Jail, with a private cell and telephone privileges. Among his visitors were aldermen and pols, gangsters from Chicago, and peers from New York—including Little John Torrio, Lucky Luciano, and Dutch Schultz. As his appeals were rejected by higher courts in the early months of 1932, Capone and the feds prepared for his transfer. With Guzik, Nitti, and others from Chicago serving their time in Leavenworth, the U.S. Bureau of Prisons sent Capone to Atlanta.

Assigned number 40,822, Capone was paired in Atlanta with safecracker Red "Rusty" Rudensky, a veteran con who befriended the gangster kingpin. During his lengthy stretches in prison Rudensky learned to write and fashioned himself as a chronicler of life behind bars. As editor of the prison newspaper, he drew attention from Atlanta novelist Margaret Mitchell and crusading editor Ralph McGill, who encouraged him to keep a diary in which Capone became a frequent subject. According to Rudensky, Al frequently suffered from nightmares that jolted him awake while yelling "No, No!" During daylight hours, Capone showed off pictures of his son: "How can a fat dago like me have a son so good-looking," Capone would joke.

With Rudensky's help, Capone arranged for thousands of dollars in cash to be smuggled inside via a trusty who drove one of the prison supply trucks. Stashing this wad in a hollowed-out broom handle, Capone and Rudensky used it to buy favors and privileges, loyalty and protection.

The two inmates spent nearly eighteen months together, until Capone was transferred to Alcatraz on August 22, 1934. Over the next four and a half years, according to prison records and Warden James A. Johnston's memoir, *Alcatraz Island and the Men Who Live There*, the Big Fella's mental and physical

Capone being escorted to Atlanta to serve his sentence.

health fell apart. First, his efforts to win favor with Johnston led to a public humiliation; second, his isolation from family and friends broke his spirit. Though he tried to fight for his sanity by obtaining a tenor banjo and learning the basic elements of musical notation, Capone floundered in the hastily formed prison band that included his fingerpicking and bank robber George "Machine Gun" Kelly's drumming behind kidnapper Harmon Waley's saxophone. After an initial period of cooperation, reported Steve Ellis in his book *Alcatraz 1172*, the band began to tear itself apart when Capone traded his instrument for a mandolin. After inmates whispered that Capone had paid $600 for the new instrument and a similar amount to import sheet music from Europe, Waley and Kelly grew skeptical of their partner. During one session, Capone asked Kelly to play at lower decibels. As soon as Al turned his back, Waley smashed the horn over the Big Fella's head. The fight landed both men in solitary confinement for a week. Afterward, Capone chose to sit in his cell and play alone.

During a protest over conditions organized by the inmates, Capone found himself in a bind. If he joined strikes or job actions, he believed the authorities would tag him as the ringleader and automatically increase his sentence. At the same time, his failure to join lowered his standing in the eyes of his fellow convicts. Keeping clear of a January 1936 protest, Al endured the taunts of his peers, who dubbed him "phony Caponi" and threatened to kill him, his wife, and his son. Though Machine Gun Kelly and other inmates understood Al's predicament, they could not discourage others from resenting the onetime gangster kingpin who was now called "The Wop with the Mop."

While the hard guys staked their claim to run the rock, Capone retreated into his music and frustrations. At times, other inmates saw him talking to the walls, acting out bold fantasies of rubouts or power grabs. When confronted or ridiculed, he broke down into whimpers and an occasional display of tears, marking him an easy target for predators. On June 23, 1936, Jimmy Lucas, a Texas outlaw, used a prison razor blade to stab Capone underneath the kidneys. Capone recovered in the prison hospital, and twelve years was added to Lucas's sentence of thirty.

The attack led to Capone's further withdrawal. Though the arrival of Alfred "Creepy" Karpis and nine other members of his gang lifted his spirits and gave him protection from additional scrapes, Capone drifted away from most of the prisoners. He spent hours and hours making and remaking his bed, singing to himself, fiddling with his musical instruments, talking to fictional characters, pretending he remained the boss, pretending he was an opera star.

On the morning of February 5, 1938, Karpis noticed that the inmate line for breakfast had begun to slow down as it passed Capone's cell. "I can see he has no idea where he is," Karpis wrote in his memoir, *Twenty-Five Years on the Rock*. "The guard is on duty watching him closely. He's dressed for the yard, not the mess hall. His work gloves have been shoved in his back pocket at the last moment and protrude from his coat."

In a stutter step that wound its way into the mess hall, Karpis observed, Capone entered way behind the line, violating the strict rules regarding an inmate keeping his place in the daily gatherings. "About half way down the aisle, Capone staggers, turns looking for help where none exists, and vomits on the dining room floor. Two screws escort him upstairs to the hospital. He never returns to population."

The initial diagnosis of advanced syphilis and psychosis with general paralysis landed Capone in one of Alcatraz's three "bug cages"—cells made of wire mesh that ran off the main corridor to the hospital ward. After a series of telegrams and desperate pleas, Mae Capone and her son settled into the laborious task of arranging a visit to the nation's most punitive penal colony. With the wardens deliberately slowing down the process, Mae and Sonny fought for more than six months to win final permission. On August 3, 1938, Al was escorted into the Alcatraz visiting area. Through the square glass peephole, he observed a young man in a summer suit, his shoulders squared. It was the first time that father and son had seen each other since their last meeting at Cook County Jail in the early months of 1932. At that time, Al was still in his tailor-made linens and silks. Now he was in denim and canvas.

"The son looked at a man wearing an ill-fitting prison uniform," wrote a United Press reporter, "and said 'Dad.'"

"Capone reached forward to embrace him. But bars and nonshatterable prison glass separated them. 'My boy,' he said."

After the perfunctory twenty-minute visit that barely went beyond pleasantries, Mae and Sonny were forced to leave, and Al returned to his cage. Though medication had kept his mood swings on a fairly even keel, Capone was agitated by the excitement of seeing his son and the despair of presenting himself in such a deranged state. Shortly after the visit, Karpis recorded a bizarre incident involving Al and a bank robber, Carl Janway, confined to another bug cage.

Through the mesh, Capone and Janway began taunting each other.

The hostility lingered for days until Janway reached for his bedpan and threw a fistful of excrement at Capone's cell. Capone drew ammunition from his own bedpan and returned fire. "Everything within range," Karpis noted, "slowly changes color as sickly green-brown lumps land indiscriminately."

After the combatants had spent their last rounds, orderlies hosed down the floor.

On November 19, 1938, the prison physicians recommended Capone's transfer to the hospital at Springfield, Missouri, or Leavenworth, Kansas. He was allowed to walk out of the prison and head for the Alcatraz ferry dock on January 6, 1939. Under armed guard, he was taken to the mainland and transported to the prison hospital at Terminal Island near Los Angeles. There he would spend another eleven months in custody. His last days of incarceration took place on a train to Pennsylvania. On the morning of November 16, 1939, he stepped out of the federal prison in Lewisburg, Pennsylvania, and found Mae and Sonny waiting in a limousine.

Al Capone would live another seven years. Settled in the Palm Island house, he shuffled between the rooms and the dock, sometimes in his pajamas, sometimes dressed in sports clothes. Occasionally, his wife and son or the two servants found him wandering in a daze and mumbling about his former days and nights as gang boss. Once in a while, he recognized a relative and had a glass of lemonade or soda. In the warm weather, Capone loved to sit with a fishing pole jigging into the bay. If he was lucid, Mae would allow him to ride on a boat.

Although the Capone and Coughlin families remained intact, Al withered away, the syphilis eating into his brain and slowly taking away his ability to speak and reason, control his limbs and gastro-intestinal system. As the end of his life approached, several of his colleagues paid their last respects. When reporters ran down Greasy Thumb Guzik, he was one of the few who refused to lie. "Al," he said, "is nuttier than a fruitcake."

Despite this hard assessment, Guzik and others remained loyal to Capone and his family. When Al celebrated his forty-

Capone was buried on February 4, 1947, in Chicago's Mount Olivet Cemetery.

eighth birthday, Greasy Thumb extended his best wishes. Two days later Capone collapsed from a brain hemorrhage.

On January 25, he passed away.

Nine days later, his casket arrived at Mount Olivet Cemetery, where Guzik and Murray "the Camel" Humphreys joined the family and a handful of other mourners in one of the underworld's smallest funerals. Ralph barked at the reporters and photographers, demanding they step back. Monsignor William Gorman, chaplain to the Chicago Fire Department, led the family and mourners through a few prayers. Then he dropped to one knee and watched the grave diggers lower Capone's coffin into a bare plot. The priest and the family never said a word to the press, but the scribes noticed that none of the hard guys had sent flowers to send off the man who made *gangster* a household word.

CHRONOLOGY

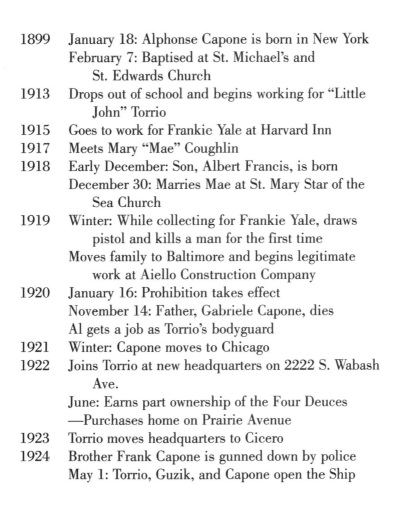

1899	January 18: Alphonse Capone is born in New York
	February 7: Baptised at St. Michael's and St. Edwards Church
1913	Drops out of school and begins working for "Little John" Torrio
1915	Goes to work for Frankie Yale at Harvard Inn
1917	Meets Mary "Mae" Coughlin
1918	Early December: Son, Albert Francis, is born
	December 30: Marries Mae at St. Mary Star of the Sea Church
1919	Winter: While collecting for Frankie Yale, draws pistol and kills a man for the first time
	Moves family to Baltimore and begins legitimate work at Aiello Construction Company
1920	January 16: Prohibition takes effect
	November 14: Father, Gabriele Capone, dies
	Al gets a job as Torrio's bodyguard
1921	Winter: Capone moves to Chicago
1922	Joins Torrio at new headquarters on 2222 S. Wabash Ave.
	June: Earns part ownership of the Four Deuces
	—Purchases home on Prairie Avenue
1923	Torrio moves headquarters to Cicero
1924	Brother Frank Capone is gunned down by police
	May 1: Torrio, Guzik, and Capone open the Ship

—Torrio leaves and taps Capone as caretaker of the organization

1925   January 24: Torrio is shot and retires as overlord

1926   July 30: Sidesteps murder rap and moves to take complete control of Chicago organized crime

September 20: Attacked at the Hawthorn Inn

1927   William "Big Bill" Thompson re-elected mayor of Chicago

1928   Purchases new home in Miami

July 1: Orders the assassination of Frankie Yale

1929   February 14: the St. Valentine's Day massacre

March 12: Subpoenaed to appear before a grand jury and questioned about financial transactions

May 13–16: Heads to Atlantic City to meet with other crime bosses in an effort to establish a national commission to mediate disputes

May 17: Has himself arrested in order to escape possible assassination attempts

1930   March 17: Released from jail

March 23: U.S. Attorney George E.Q. Johnson announces the tax evasion indictment and trial of Ralph Capone

Al Capone hires tax specialist Lawrence Mattingly to help strike a deal

1931   October 17: Jury finds Capone guilty of three felonies for tax evasion and two misdemeanors for failing to file an income tax return

October 24: Sentenced to eleven years in jail

1934   August 22: Transferred to Alcatraz

1936   June 23: Stabbed by fellow inmate

1939   January 6: Transferred out of Alcatraz on medical orders

November 16: Released from federal prison and reunited with family

1946   January 25: Dies from the effects of syphilis

BIBLIOGRAPHY

BOOKS

Allsop, Kenneth. *The Bootleggers and Their Era*. Garden City, N.Y.: Doubleday, 1961.

Asbury, Herbert. *The Gangs of New York*. New York: Alfred A. Knopf, 1928.

———— *Gem of the Prairie: An Informational History of the Chicago Underworld*. New York: Alfred A. Knopf, 1940.

———— *The Great Illusion: An Informal History of Prohibition*, Garden City, N.Y.: Doubleday, 1950.

Balsamo, William and George Carpozi Jr. *Under the Clock: The Inside Story of the Mafia's First Hundred Years*, Far Hills, N.J.: New Horizon Press, 1988.

Bergreen, Laurence. *Capone: The Man and the Era*. New York: Simon & Schuster, 1994.

Brenner, Teddy and Barney Nagler. *Only the Ring Was Square*. Englewood Cliffs, N.J.: Prentice Hall, 1981.

Breslin, Jimmy. *Damon Runyon*. New York: Ticknor & Fields, 1991.

Cooper, Courtney Ryley. *Ten Thousand Public Enemies*. Boston: Little Brown, 1935.

Ellis, Steve. *Alcatraz Number 1172*. Los Angeles: Holloway House, 1972.

Fetherling, Doug. *The Five Lives of Ben Hecht*. Toronto: Lester and Orpen, 1977.

Fox, Stephen. *Blood and Power: Organized Crime in Twentieth Century America*. New York: Penguin Books, 1989.

Fraley, Oscar and Paul Robsky. *The Last of the Untouchables*. New York: Pocket Books, 1988.

Halper, Albert, ed. *The Chicago Crime Book*. Cleveland: World Publishing, 1967.

Harrison, Carter H. *Stormy Years: The Autobiography of Carter Harrison*. Indianapolis: Bobbs-Merrill, 1935.

Hecht, Ben. *A Child of the Century*. New York: Simon & Schuster, 1954.

Hinton, Milt and David G. Berger. *Bass Line: The Stories and Photographs of Milton Hinton*. Philadelphia: Temple University Press, 1988.

Hoover, Herbert. *The Memoirs of Herbert Hoover: The Cabinet and the Presidency, 1920–1933*. New York: Macmillan, 1952.

Irey, Elmer and William Slocum. *The Tax Dodgers: The Inside Story of the T-Men's War with America's Political and Underworld Hoodlums*. New York: Greenberg, 1948.

Karpis, Alvin. *On the Rock: Twenty-Five Years in Alcatraz*. Mississauga, Ontario: L. B. S. Inc., 1988.

Kobler, John. *Ardent Spirits: The Rise and Fall of Prohibition*. New York: G. P. Putnam's Sons, 1973.

——— *Capone: The Life and World of Al Capone*. New York: G. P. Putnam's Sons, 1971.

Landesco, John. *Organized Crime in Chicago: Part III of the Illinois Crime Survey*. Chicago: University of Chicago Press, 1929.

Lindberg, Richard. *Chicago Ragtime: Another Look at Chicago, 1880–1920*. South Bend, Indiana: Icaruf, 1985.

Lyle, John H. *The Dry and Lawless Years*. Englewood Cliffs, N.J.: Prentice Hall, 1960.

McPhaul, John J. *Deadline and Monkeyshines: The Fabled World of Chicago Journalism*. Englewood Cliffs, N.J.: Prentice Hall, 1962.

——— *Johnny Torrio: The First of the Gang Lords*. New Rochelle, N.Y.: Arlington House, 1970.

Mezzrow, Muzz and Bernard Wolfe. *Really the Blues*. Garden City, N.Y.: Doubleday, 1972.

Murray, George. *The Legacy of Al Capone: Portraits and Annals of Chicago's Public Enemies*. New York: Putnam's, 1975.

Nash, Jay Robert. *Bloodletter and Badmen*. New York: M. Evans, 1973.

——— *Encyclopedia of World Crime, 6 vols*. Wilmette, Ill.: Crime Books, 1989.

Nelli, Humbert. *The Italians in Chicago, 1889–1939*. New York: Oxford University Press, 1970.

——— *The Business of Crime: Italians and Syndicate Crimes in the*

United States. New York: Oxford University Press, 1976.

———— *From Immigrants to Ethnics: The Italian Americans*. New York: Oxford University Press, 1983.

Ness, Eliot and Oscar Fraley. *The Untouchables*. New York: Popular Library, 1960.

Pasley, Fred. *Al Capone: The Biography of a Self-Made Man*. New York: Garden City Publishing, 1930.

Ross, Robert. *The Trial of Al Capone*. Chicago: Robert Ross, 1933.

Rudensky, Morris and Don Riley. *The Gonif*, Blue Earth, Minnesota: Piper, 1970.

Runyon, Damon. *Trials and Tribulations*. Philadelphia: Lippincott, 1947.

St. John, Robert. *This Was My World*. Garden City, N.Y.: Doubleday, 1953.

Sifakis, Carl. *The Mafia Encyclopedia*. New York: Facts on File, 1987.

Smith, Alson. *Chicago's Left Bank*. Chicago: Henry Regnery, 1953.

———— *Syndicate City: The Chicago Crime Cartel*. Chicago: Henry Regnery, 1954.

Sullivan, Edward Dean. *Chicago Surrenders*. New York: Vanguard Press, 1930.

———— *Rattling the Cup of Chicago Crime*. New York: Vanguard Press, 1929.

Thompson, Erwin. *The Rock: A History of Alcatraz Island, 1847–1972*. Denver: National Park Service, 1972.

United States, Bulletin to the Department of Labor, The Padrone System and Padrone Banks.

National Archives Files of the United States Department of Justice, Federal Bureau of Investigation, Bureau of Prisons, and court papers pertaining to Alphonse and Ralph Capone.

Waller, Irle. *Chicago Uncensored*. New York: Exposition Press, 1965.

Wendt, Lloyd and Herman Kogan. *Big Bill of Chicago*. Indianapolis: Bobbs-Merrill, 1953.

Wilson, Frank and Beth Day. *Special Agent: A Quarter Century with the Treasury Department and the Secret Service*. New York: Holt, Rinehart, and Winston, 1965.

Woodford, Jack and Neil Elliot. *My Years With Capone*. Seattle: Woodford Memorial Editions, 1985.

PERIODICALS

Collier's

Chicago Herald & Examiner

Chicago Tribune

L.A. Times

Miami Daily News

New Republic

New York Times

North American Review

SOURCES

CHAPTER ONE
REFERENCES

Bergreen; Fetherling; Kobler; Nelli; *New Republic*; *New York Times*; *North American Review*; Sifikis; *United States, Bulletin to the Department of Labor*; Woodford.

SOURCES

p. 3 *42,977 Italians who*: Nelli, pp. 18–22.

p. 4 *For wages that averaged*: United States, Bulletin to the Department of Labor.

p. 5 *"swarthy, sullen"*: Kobler, p. 25.

p. 7 *"When he found"* and ensuing: Woodford, p. 7.

p. 8 *a pattern of truancy*: Kobler, pp. 26–28.

p. 9 *Everybody in the*: ibid.

p. 9 *While enlisting a boxer*: Sifikis, p. 121.

p. 10 *"This band of hooligans"*: New York Times, March 28, 1900.

p. 11 *Having barely made it*: Bergreen, pp. 35–36.

p. 13 *"something of a non-entity"*: New Republic, September 9, 1931.

p. 13 *"never drank and"*: North American Review, September 1929.

p. 14 *"an excellent dancer"*: New Republic, September 9, 1931.

p. 17 *"Honey, you have a nice"*: Bergreen, pp. 49–51.

p. 20 *"From the beginning"* and ensuing: Fetherling, p. 106.

p. 20 *On Garfield Place*: Bergreen, p. 52.

p. 21 *"He thought prostitutes"*: Woodford, p. 79.

p. 21 *"Mae was different"*: Bergreen, p. 52.

p. 24 *"How else could he"*: Woodford, p. 45.

CHAPTER TWO

REFERENCES

Asbury; Harrison; Kobler; Lyle; Mezzrow and Wolfe; Pasley; Waller; Wendt and Kogan; Woodford.

SOURCES

p. 31 *"Here they could rub"* and ensuing: Harrison, p. 305.

p. 32 *"He was just one of"*: Woodford, p. 2.

p. 32 *"Looking quiet and thoughtful"*: ibid.

p. 34 *"The girls we knew"* and ensuing: Mezzrow and Wolfe, pp. 51–54.

p. 35 *"with part of a hairy"*: Waller, p. 67.

p. 35 *"Chicago's arch criminal"*: Quoted in Asbury, p. 341.

p. 37 *"I saw him there"*: Quoted in Kobler, p. 67.

p. 37 *"I got some firsthand"* and ensuing: Lyle, p. 74.

p. 39 *"This was an indulgence"*: Woodford, p. 4.

p. 40 *"Johnny came to know"*: ibid, p. 2.

p. 42 *"Alfred Caponi . . ."*: quoted in Pasley, p. 20.

p. 43 *"The bad breath of"*: Wendt and Kogan, p. 237.

p. 43 *"To hell with the public"*: Kobler, p. 111.

p. 45 *"Collins, there's a dry law"*: ibid.

p. 47 *"I can whip this bird"*: ibid, p. 108.

p. 47 *"Whenever Al was wanted"*: Woodford, p. 70.

CHAPTER THREE

REFERENCES

Bergreen; Hinton; Kobler; Lyle; Pasley; St. John; Smith; Woodford.

SOURCES

p. 50 *"all my peers"* and ensuing: Hinton, pp. 21–23.

p. 53 *"The Capones owned the"*: Smith, p. 211.

p. 53 *"To them, it was"*: ibid, pp. 211-212.

p. 56 *Everything was in place*: Bergreen, pp. 112-113.

p. 56 *"a dirty little kike"*: ibid, p. 112.

p. 56 *"Listen, you dago pimp"*: Lyle, p. 13.

p. 56 *"I am certain it was"*: Pasley, p. 27.

p. 57 *"I hear the police"*: Bergreen, p. 114.

p. 57 *"bullets fired from"*: Pasley, p. 30.

p. 61 *"Hello Boys, you"*: Kobler, p. 129.

p. 61 *"Mr. O'Banion called"*: ibid.

p. 62 *"If I knew who had killed"*: ibid, p. 132.

p. 62 *"Deany was all right"*: ibid, pp. 132-133.

p. 65 *"You're the man"* and ensuing: ibid, p. 137.

p. 66 *"the only friend"*: Woodford, p. 31.

p. 69 *"This is the last raid"*: *Chicago Tribune*, October 8, 1931.

p. 70 *"Sure I got a racket"*: St. John, pp. 194–97.

p. 70 *"Well, Mr. Publisher"*: ibid.

p. 72 *"Why didn't you stop?"*: Kobler, p. 157.

p. 72 *"Take that, you son"*: ibid, p. 158.

p. 73 *"Our members are"*: ibid, p. 35.

p. 74 *"these men will"*: ibid, p. 158.

p. 75 *"The verdict is a blow"*: Kobler, p. 161.

CHAPTER FOUR

REFERENCES

Allsop; Balsamo and Carpozi; Bergreen; Kobler; Pasley; Wendt and Kogan; Woodford.

SOURCES

p. 78 *"I'll give you $100,000"*: Balsamo and Carpozi, p. 202.

p. 80 *"Chicago is unique"* and ensuing: ibid, p. 63.

p. 83 *"my friend Billy"*: Pasley, p. 132.

p. 83 *"if I told"*: Kobler, p. 128.

p. 85 *"I paid McSwiggin at"*: ibid, p. 182.

p. 85 *"Subsequent information"*: Pasley, p. 132.

p. 86 *"They were after my roll"*: ibid, pp. 119–24.

p. 87 *"It's a stall boss"*: ibid, pp. 113–14.

p. 88 *"He's a snake"* and ensuing: Bergreen, p. 207.

p. 88 *"Scalise and Anselmi"*: ibid.

p. 89 *"I wouldn't do that"*: Kobler, p. 187.

p. 91 *"All I ever did was"*: Pasley, pp. 349-350.

p. 92 *"It's a waste of time"*: Kobler, p. 190.

p. 94 *"I told them we're making"*: Allsop, p. 125.

p. 95 *"I'm wetter than the"*: Kobler, p. 199.

p. 96 *"To Al, this chair"*: Woodford, p. 81.

p. 97 *"to vote early and"*: Bergreen, pp. 218–24.

p. 98 *"I'll get you"* and ensuing: Pasley, p. 160.

p. 101 *"Big Bill Thompson"* Wendt and Kogan, p. 32.

p. 102 *"Capone didn't order"* and ensuing: Woodford, p. 85.

p. 102 *"My God, what"*: Kobler, p. 203

p. 103 *"After this"*: Woodford, p. 86.

CHAPTER FIVE

REFERENCES

Bergreen; *Chicago Herald & Examiner*; *Chicago Sun Times*; *Chicago Tribune*; Hecht; Kobler; *L.A. Times*; McPhaul; *Miami Daily News*; *New York Times*; Woodford.

SOURCES

p. 106 *"Sweat ice water"*: Kobler, p. 272.

p. 107 *"It is the wish"*: ibid, p. 205.

p. 109 *"You're dead, friend"* and ensuing: ibid, p. 207.

p. 110 *"I'm the boss"*: ibid, pp. 207-208

p. 111 *"I've been spending"*: *Chicago Tribune*, December 6, 1927.

p. 111 *"There's one thing"*: Kobler, p. 209.

p. 111 *"Let the worthy citizens"*: *Chicago Tribune*, December 6, 1927.

p. 112 *"I thought you"* and ensuing: *L.A. Times*, December 14, 1927.

p. 112 *"Pleased to meet"* and ensuing: *Chicago Herald & Examiner*, December 17, 1927.

p. 113 *"He knew how our"*: McPhaul, p. 106.

p. 113 *"He knew that we"*: ibid.

p. 113 *"Sure the stories"*: *Chicago Sun Times*, January 25, 1967.

p. 113 *"On many occasions"*: ibid.

p. 114 *"another sucker"* and ensuing: *Chicago Tribune*, January 12, 1928.

p. 118 *"The criminal element"*: Kobler, p. 218.

p. 119 *"The police are with us"*: ibid, p. 221.

p. 120 *"moral detriment"*: *Miami Daily News*, June 27, 1928.

CHAPTER SIX

REFERENCES

Allsop; Bergreen; *Chicago Tribune; Collier's;* Kobler; Linberg; Lyle; Murray; *New York Times*; Pasley; Woodford.

SOURCES

p. 124 *"completely anonymous"*: *Collier's*, April 26, 1947.

p. 124 *"I have been able to"* and ensuing: ibid.

p. 131 *"Nobody shot me"* and ensuing: Pasley, pp. 256–57.

p. 133 *"only Capone kills like"* and ensuing: Linberg, p. 201.

p. 136 *"They say the police"*: *Chicago Tribune*, March 6, 1929.

p. 136 *"split the difference"*: *Chicago Tribune*, March 21–22, 1929.

p. 137 *"This is what we"* and ensuing: Lyle, pp. 221–22.

p. 139 *"There are two ways"*: Bergreen, p. 334.

p. 139 *"Al's rise was meteoric"*: Woodford, p. 17.

p. 141 *"In none of the"*: Quoted in Bergreen, p. 365.

p. 142 *"I don't understand"*: Allsop, pp. 314–16.

p. 143 *"Mr. Mattingly has called"* and ensuing: Bergreen, p. 365.

p. 144 *"Organized crime was"*: *New York Times*, April 3, 1932.

p. 145 *"Well of all the"*: Bergreen, p. 421.

p. 146 *"The men with power"* and ensuing: Murray, p. 343.

p. 146 *"He got put away"*: Woodford, p. 127.

p. 149 *"I'm being tailed"*: Kobler, p. 289.

CHAPTER SEVEN

REFERENCES

Bergreen; *Collier's*; Irey; Karpis; Kobler; *New York Times*.

SOURCES

p. 154 *"Frank paid $17,000"*: *Collier's*, April 26, 1947.

p. 158 *"Your proposal to"*: Bergreen, p. 434.

p. 159 *"It is time"*: *New York Times*, September 31, 1931.

p. 161 *"It was a smashing blow"*: *New York Times*, October 25, 1931.

p. 161 *"You look like a wop"*: Irey, p. 65.

p. 162 *"How can a fat dago"*: Kobler, p. 351.

p. 163 *"The Wop with the"*: Bergreen, p. 341.

p. 164 *"I can see he has"* and ensuing: Karpis, pp. 101–02.

p. 164 *"About half way down"*: ibid.

p. 165 *"The son looked at"*: Bergreen, p. 562.

p. 165 *"Everything within range"*: Karpis, pp. 118–19.

p. 166 *"is nuttier than a"*: Kobler, p. 373.

PHOTOGRAPHY CREDITS

pp. iv, 49 courtesy of UPI/Corbis-Bettmann

pp. 1, 76 courtesy of UPI/Corbis-Bettmann

pp. 2, 27 courtesy of AP/Wide World Photos

pp. 3, 104 courtesy of UPI/Corbis-Bettmann

p. 8 courtesy of Archive Photos

p. 16 © New York Times Co./Archive Photos

p. 19 courtesy of Archive Photos

p. 23 courtesy of AP/ Wide World Photos

p. 26 courtesy of UPI/Corbis-Bettmann

p. 30 courtesy of Archive Photos

p. 33 courtesy of Archive Photos

p. 38 courtesy of AP/Wide World Photos

p. 48 courtesy of UPI/Corbis-Bettmann

p. 59 courtesy of UPI/Corbis-Bettmann

p. 65 courtesy of Archive Photos

p. 67 © American Stock/Archive Photos

pp. 77, 122 courtesy of UPI/Corbis-Bettmann

p. 84 courtesy of UPI/Corbis-Bettmann

p. 99 courtesy of AP/Wide World Photos

p. 100 courtesy of UPI/Corbis-Bettmann

pp. 105, 159 courtesy of UPI/Corbis-Bettmann

p. 108 courtesy of Archive Photos

p. 115 courtesy of AP/Wide World Photos

p. 118 courtesy of AP/Wide World Photos

pp. 123, 134 courtesy of UPI/Corbis-Bettmann

p. 129 courtesy of UPI/Corbis-Bettmann

p. 132 courtesy of Archive Photos

p. 150 courtesy of AP/Wide World Photos

p. 152 courtesy of Archive Photos

pp. 153, 162 courtesy of AP/Wide World Photos

p. 156 courtesy of UPI/Corbis-Bettmann

p. 167 courtesy of AP/Wide World Photos

INDEX

ACKNOWLEDGMENTS

This book could not have been written without the generous support and help of Tom Dyja and Irene Agriodimas at Balliett & Fitzgerald, the good humor of Dr. David Carter, Dr. Stanley Battle, Floyd Bagwell, Margaret Hebert, Fran Tremblay, Carmen Morales and my colleagues at the Learning Center of Eastern Connecticut State University. I am also extremely thankful for the wise council of Simon Potter and Steven Pasternak, the keen insight of Chris Calhoun, and the kindness of Alison Reid.

Throughout the writing of this book, George, Dorothy and Richard Palmer offered all kinds of assistance and guidance. Their contributions serve as an immense gift.

I owe a special thanks to my brother Mark, Jaqueline Pardo, Daniel and Max Hornung, who embody the vibrant gusts of the windy city. And finally words cannot express my gratitude to Peggy Palmer, Sarah and Gabriel Hornung, who helped me fulfill the dream about writing a book about my hometown.

ABOUT THE AUTHOR

Rick Hornung is a veteran journalist and reporter who has written for *The New York Times*, *The Village Voice*, *The Chicago Tribune*, *The Boston Phoenix*, and *The Atlanta Constitution*, among others. His most recent book is *One Nation Under the Gun*. He lives in Connecticut.